THE AC
SMALL

Tales from Spillers Farm

BRIDGET TRAYLING

FOR KEITH

Without him, none of this would have happened

LIVING THE DREAM

The man looked up at me, removed his sunglasses, smiled lazily and said, "You're living my dream", returned his sunglasses to his nose and gazed out again over the tearoom lawns taking in the beautiful view on a perfect, sunny Devonshire afternoon.

I put down the tray loaded with a cream tea for two: cups and saucers, plates, knives, napkins, a large pot of tea, milk, four large homemade scones, our own homemade raspberry jam made from our homegrown raspberries and, of course, the ubiquitous clotted cream, straightened up and said:

"I got up at five this morning, crept past the other bedrooms so as not to disturb the sleeping B&B guests who wouldn't get up for another three hours, prepared the bottles to bottle feed our lambs for the first of their three feeds today, then fed our fifty hens, collected at least a dozen eggs, laid the tables for breakfast, washed up from the night before, made..oh, I don't know... probably four or more cakes for the tearoom as well as homemade soup, a daily special (hot meal and pudding), made salad to serve with the lunchtime sandwiches, served eight breakfasts, not forgetting to chat to all the guests and remember their names as well as details about their lives, washed up from breakfast, waved goodbye to the guests, stripped their beds, cleaned their rooms, picked their pubic hairs from out of the shower plugholes, made the rooms up, washed up again, prepared the bottles to feed the lambs for lunchtime, opened the tearoom, served teas, coffees, cakes, lunches, made umpteen more scones for the afternoon cream tea rush. I haven't eaten, sat down or had a cup of tea in hours. I've needed to pee for at least the last 45 minutes but haven't yet had time and will probably only get to go in about 20 minutes when my bladder actually feels like it's bursting. I will be working until 10 tonight and by the time I crawl exhaustedly back into bed I'll be so footsore my feet will be throbbing with pain. And then I'll get up tomorrow and do it all over again. You, however, are sitting in MY garden, relaxing on this perfect afternoon, without having to worry about people asking you to bring them another cup because the one they've got apparently smells of fish. You are living MY dream."

This never happened of course. Well, a woman did once ask for a replacement cup as she thought it smelt of fish. (It was the dishwasher tablets. I never put a fish in a cup). And someone did once tell me I was living their dream. I just smiled.

He had no idea how much bloody hard work his 'dream' was.

So, to all those people who think I was living their dream, I have this to say.

I'm sorry. I didn't mean to.

ACKNOWLEDGMENTS

My thanks to Jim and Gill for the cups of tea and loan of their lovely PC.
Also special thanks to Glyn Dewis for his permission to use some of his wonderful photographs.

To all the friends and family and friends that have now become family, and anyone who came to stay with us at Spillers Farm. Thank you for helping us to live someone else's dream.

All mistakes regarding farming practices, procedures etc (and there are bound to be hundreds, I never really knew what I was doing) are completely my own.

Please note that for privacy reasons the names of some of the humans in this book have been changed. The animals' names, however, are all their own. Except one of the pigs.

TEAROOM NOVICES

We first saw Spillers Farm on a drab and dull November day in 2004 and instantly fell in love. Keith and I had been married for just over two years and had left London on a whim and a prayer with a desire to live in the countryside, but not much of an idea of how or where. Having left our jobs in London we had a vague idea that wherever we ended up would have to provide us with an income but that was about as far as we had got in terms of planning.

But Spillers was perfect. A farmhouse situated just inside the borders of three counties – Devon,

Dorset and Somerset – with 14 acres of land in three different fields, an existing small business in a tearoom, an annexed three-bedroom cottage, and a small Caravan Club CL (Certified Location) site would be enough to get us started. And we could see the potential for B&B as one of the rooms was en-suite. To top it all there was a lake in one of the fields. Well, back then it was more or less a big hole dug in the ground by the previous owners, that had filled with water because of the low water table, but like everything else we saw that day, it had potential. Coming from West London, 14 acres was about the same size as our local park, and it seemed enormous. We couldn't believe it could all be ours. Well, ours and the bank's. In fact, mostly the bank's. In those heady days of the early 2000's banks were handing out money like it was going out of fashion. It has. But, with a business plan almost literally scratched on the bag of a fag packet and no real idea of what we were doing, the bank handed us almost £400k and our 'escape to the country' had begun.

To celebrate we went to the local seaside town of Seaton. This was the weekend before Christmas and in London the shops would have been bursting at the seams. Police would have been yelling instructions through loudspeakers at the enormous crowds about crossing Oxford Street. It was 3.30 in the afternoon, there was a chilly fog descending in the growing twilight and Seaton High Street was absolutely deserted. The only sound was a crackly rendition of Silent Night from a small speaker hoisted above one of the empty shops. For the first – but not the last – time, we looked at each other and wondered what on earth we had just done.

We moved in a few months' later on the Friday of the late May Bank Holiday weekend, and pretty much spent that entire weekend putting together flat-pack furniture. I also spent the weekend trying to calm the panic in my head by making cakes and scones and learning what might be required on a country tearoom menu. Finding that I hadn't brough half enough flour for this venture, I drove to the local supermarket in Axminster only to find that it was Bank Holiday Monday and wouldn't open for hours. What kind of backwater was this I panicked? The kind of backwater I would come to adore. But all that was to come. When we finally opened the tearoom doors on the afternoon of 25th May 2005, and the first car almost immediately drove in, I was shaking like a leaf. It's all very well making a cake for a friend but making one for a complete stranger and then asking them for £2.50 for a slice is a completely different matter!

But nobody seemed to notice that we were novices. The weather was good, and they came in droves. They came in such numbers that my mother spent the entire afternoon making batch after batch of scones (the supermarket having eventually opened for me to re-stock) and everyone seemed happy to pay us to eat them. It was a revelation. Little did they seem to know, or care, that their authentic Devonshire Cream Tea was being served by a former Londoner who just six months prior had been a builder. As long as the sun shone, people wanted a cream tea and we made them hand over fist, fist over hand, for hours on end, days on end, weeks on end. According to that font of all rumours, lies and scurrilous accusations Wikipedia, the origin of the cream tea is disputed, but there is evidence of bread with cream and jam being eaten by the monks of Tavistock Abbey in the 11th century. All I have to say, thank Friar Tuck for that, because the Devon Cream Tea is the most marvellous piece of marketing. (Just lost any readers from Cornwall. The Devon/Cornish Cream Tea argument is almost as old and as intense as the jam first/cream first debate. I'm sticking with the idea that it originated in Devon because Spillers was just over the Devon border from both Dorset and Somerset, giving us the opportunity to claim that customers were having the first – or last – cream tea in Devon.)

Another revelation was the AGA. I'd never seen one before, and the one in Spillers' kitchen was a behemoth. A great big, four-door oven which was never turned off. I burnt myself often in the early days, but quickly learned that I couldn't live without an AGA. The constant and consistent temperature was perfect for baking and for making perfectly cooked eggs on the top plate. An AGA-cooked breakfast is a truly wonderful thing and we soon learned to use it to our advantage.

One of the joys of the four-door AGA is the warming oven which will keep food warm for hours. We learned to cook the breakfast in advance with all the components waiting in the warming oven for when the guests finally arose, with just the eggs to do as the finishing touch. And here's another secret. If anyone asked us for scrambled or poached eggs, my indomitable, charmer husband would always talk them out of it. You can cook an egg straight onto the hotplate on the top of an AGA. It looks like a fried egg, but it's cooked with no fat, just the heat of the plate. So somehow Keith always managed to persuade everyone that was what they wanted. Keith had a habit of persuading people that they somehow wanted what he wanted. It probably explains why we are married. It might explain how we ended up in Devon and it definitely explains how I ended up as a smallholder.

TROTTERS' BOTTOM

'I want to get a pig.' Two months into our time at Spillers, Keith announced this desire while we were sitting in the kitchen one day. I was astonished and a little bit scared. I was quite scared of every animal that wasn't a cat or a dog and was only just adjusting to this new life surrounded by scary countryside creatures. 'What on earth for?' was my incredulous reply. Little did I then realise how much I was going to love pigs - such wonderful, fun, intelligent creatures.

Our first two pigs were a pair of weaners from a nearby farm. They were brought to us one day and left to snuffle around in a makeshift outdoor run/sty. I say sty, I mean bit of tin held together with string. It was a very Heath Robinson affair and held tight to the smallholders' idiom of 'If you can't make it, cobble it together with what you've got lying around or borrow it, you might have to buy it." This 'sty' was very much of the cobble-it-together style, as was most of Spillers by the time we were finished. The previous owners of Spillers had been antiques and curios dealers and had left all sorts of bits and bobs lying around when they left, including an old railway station sign which read 'Trotters' Bottom'. Naturally, this was placed at the entrance to the sty and led to us subsequently naming all our other pigs after characters in 'Only Fools and Horses'. But for now, the two un-named weaners became our new fascination. I say 'our', I mean Keith. I was not really enamoured with them. Wary, nervous and scared would be a better way to describe how I felt about them. I watched them from a distance convinced that one day they would try to make a run for it and somehow contrive to kill me in the process. Feeding them, cleaning them out and caring for the pigs was definitely Keith's job. Encouraged by Keith, I tried once but it was not a happy process. For me, or the pigs.

Pigs are quite vocal creatures. They make a series of squeals, grunts - almost barks sometimes - throughout the day depending on their mood or what they're trying to communicate. Over the years I learned to be quite fluent in pig and would never enter the sty without grunting at them first in a sort of 'Hello-my-lovelies-who-wants-a-scratch-behind-the-ear?' sort of way, but that first encounter was very different. Nervously grasping the bucket of food, I tried to open the sty gate and that's when the squealing started. Pigs are food-orientated creatures and feeding time is one of the most exciting and therefore noisiest parts of their day. Feeding is always accompanied by much exciting squealing and frothing at the mouth. Also, they are keen to get on with the process, so one nervous amateur smallholder shouting as much as they are, trying both to open the gate and hold a bucket of food above their heads, is pretty much just getting in their way. Eager to get at the food, they started nudging the bucket before I'd got through the gate. I'm shouting at Keith, that I'm scared, doesn't he care I'm going to die here and he's shouting back telling me to pull myself together and get through the gate. The pigs were shouting, we want our food, why don't you just get through the gate, and trying to take the bucket out of my shaking hands with their heads. In the end I think I tipped the food all over the floor and fled, vowing I would never enter a sty again. But, by the end of ten years, I would happily have spent a night curled up with them all on the straw.

There's a lot of curling up on the straw with pigs. If there's nothing else for them to do, they will sleep. Their mantra seems to be, why stand when you can lie down? Why lie down when you can sleep? In the very early days, Keith would stand watching them sleep and get quite frustrated that they weren't more active. He would regularly lean over the edge of their sty and tell them to "Get up!".

Keith is very much a do-er and rarely stops to take breath. I think he was disappointed the pigs weren't the same. I don't know what made him think that pigs would be industrious animals. Pigs are delicious because they're fat and they get fat from lying around. Well, ours did. I shudder to think what commercial pigs are fed on to make them fat.

When the time came for them to fulfil their destiny as sausages and bacon, we asked our neighbour (a proper farmer named Edward) to take them to slaughter for us. We were looking forward to eating the meat we had raised, but we certainly weren't up to the dirty work of taking them to their deaths - not yet anyway.

Edward returned from the slaughterhouse carrying a very large plastic bag with something bloody inside. He plonked the bag and its contents in our sink where he was joined by Keith. He told us that inside the bag were 'the lights', basically the heart, lungs and liver of the two slaughtered pigs. 'I normally roasts 'em up and gives 'em to my dog as a treat,' he said, pulling one of the 'the lights' out of the bag by the oesophagus. 'Oh, who normally does that then?' asked Keith as - almost as one - they both turned to look at me standing (slightly horrified) at the other end of the kitchen.

I realised then that this was a job for a 'Farmer's Wife', and so taking the bull by the horns (or rather the pig by the oesophagus), I took the (still warm) inner neck of the recently deceased porcine and pulled the bloody organs out of the bag, slapped them down on a chopping board and started dissecting.

I won't say I ever really enjoyed doing the lights, but I got used to it over the years. And I certainly haven't ever tasted liver quite like it. Liver that was so fresh was an absolute delight; soft, almost marshmallowy in texture and - because it could be flash fried in a matter of minutes - what I liked to call 'fast food'. I became quite adept at separating the liver and the heart, slicing the liver into portions and bagging it all up for the freezer. We could never quite bring ourselves to eat the lungs (too soft and squidgy), but we roasted then up for our dog Merryck and he had no objections.

And so, from that moment on, we were hooked. The pigs had been fun, easy to look after and - best of all - delicious. It was time to move on a stage and get a breeding sow.

CASSIE PIG

They were huge. And I mean, really huge. They were hungry. And I mean really hungry. Slavering, squealing, foaming at the mouth hungry. And I wouldn't have put it past any of them to have taken a bite out of my quivering legs. I mean, fair's fair. It's happened to them often enough.

We had taken the plunge and actually bought a proper livestock trailer. This now signified our official entrance into the world of 'The Smallholder'. We were the proud owners of a medium sized genuine Ifor Williams. We had decided to get a real trailer (with a roof) after a frustrating and (with the distance of several years) hilarious few hours trying to herd and load our second pair of weaners.

There are two points to note when you are trying to load weaners.

Point One. Never try to make a pig go where he doesn't want to go.

Point Two. Always have a roof on the trailer.

Actually, there are two other points.

Point Three. Pigs are clever.

Point Four. Pigs are fast.

We had met a couple who lived in the village half a mile away from Spillers. Lyn and Rudi came to help clear pond weed from the lake in return for the opportunity for Rudi to dangle his rod and try to catch the fish in the lake. Seemed reasonable enough. After all, he'd put the fish in there in the first place. So, when the time came to take our second lot of weaners to 'market', we recruited their help in putting them in the trailer. We thought four of us, two of them. It'll be easy. We'll just pick them up and put them in.

We'd borrowed a trailer we thought would fit the bill - a flat-bed trailer of the type you see landscape gardeners and tree surgeons using. No roof because branches, sticks and leaves don't often try

to clamber out the of trailer whilst it's in motion.
We'd thrown a bit of tarpaulin over the top to make
a 'roof' in the way that novice smallholders from
London might do, because we imagined that a bit of
tarpaulin would have the same effect on the pig that
a cover has on a birdcage.

Three hours in and we were all exhausted. All
except the pigs who seemed to have boundless
energy. We had chased the pigs, run after the
pigs, shouted at the pigs, fallen over in the mud
(think Margo Leadbetter), got stuck in the mud,
repeat, repeat for hours, only to have them slip
through our hands time and time again. I had no
idea how fast they could run, and they can turn on
a sixpence. You have to admire them really. The
pig is an incredibly intelligent animal and if they
could laugh, they would have been literally belly
laughing at our pathetic attempts to catch them.

I don't remember how, but somehow, we eventually
got them into the trailer and Keith set off to the
abattoir. Only to find that the pigs were trying to
climb out. It would seem that they were not fooled
by the tarpaulin. Budgies they are not.

And so, a proper trailer was sourced and
purchased. Just in time to purchase our first sow.
And here we were staring at a slavering mound of
screaming pigs - each one the size of a bull to my
mind - and attempting to get one into our trailer.
This time it was a lot easier. If there is one

motivating factor to the pig it is food, and these pigs were starving. They had been bought by a couple for their daughter, who had 'fallen in love' with 12 piglets. Yes, that's right, 12. Eight sows and four boars. But naively, they had not realised how quickly pigs grow and how much they eat. Before they knew it, they had 12 full-grown pigs on their hands and not enough money to feed them, so they were trying to get rid and quickly. The pigs were being held back by a couple of strands of barbed wire and not much else. Turning our backs on them (with me desperately trying not to picture the Pamplona Bull Run), we opened the trailer door and threw in a bit of food. And then....

CHARGE!

They flew at us. One pig was in. We slammed the trailer door shut. The other poor pigs were pushed back (by the owner... I was a good six feet away) and we had our breeding sow. Although at the time I wasn't convinced it was a pig. I thought it was more like some sort of starving monster that would be coming for me with a menacing and hungry look in its eye. As I said to Keith as we drove home with the trailer rocking, "I don't know what that is, but it's not a pig."

Working on the Only Fools and Horses theme, we called her Cassandra or Cassie Pig, and somehow it really suited her. She was a Wessex Saddleback probably about 18 months old and the largest land animal I had ever seen. She stood about 4 foot high by about 6 foot long. Apparently sows continue to grow until they have their first litter and seeing as Cassie had not yet met a boar, she was big. When we expanded our herd to include other sows Cassie still stood above them. Even though she was quite underweight, if she stood on your foot, you'd know about it. Compared to the weaners she was a quiet pig, minding her own business, happy to have been rescued and just getting on with life.

After a few months of fattening her up to get her in condition we started to look for signs that she might be coming into season. We had read that when a pig is in season her (clears throat) lady bits engorge and become pinker. Unfortunately for us, Cassie was a Saddleback, meaning that her markings went something like this: big black bit at the front, pink bit in the middle and big black bit at the back. Her lady bits were therefore under her tail (just like us ladies) at the back and in the black section. How were we to know if her bits were pinker, if they were black? Or getting bigger if you could barely make them out in the first place? So, we did the obvious thing and started to photograph them, reckoning that we would be able to compare the photos each day and have some idea of what was going on down there! Can you imagine the looks we would have got if someone had been casually flicking through our photos and came upon image after image of a literal pigs' arse?! I can.

After a few weeks of collecting what I took to calling 'Pig Porn' we thought something might have happened and we took her to meet the boar who would be her boyfriend for a few years, another Saddleback called Rambo. It was only when I saw Rambo that I realised Cassie was a girl. Massive as she was, she was no match for Rambo and beside him she looked quite feminine.

Adult pigs come into season every three weeks, so we left her visiting Rambo for a month to let them get on with things and when we returned, they were rooting about in the field together. From a distance we called out: "Cassie, Cassie.". She stopped rooting, looked up and came running towards us. I told you pigs are clever. They know their names.

We had many pigs over the years, but Cassie will always have a special place in our hearts. She was our first and indeed she was first among equals. She always stood patiently waiting at her feeing station, not squealing and trying to knock the food bucket out of Keith's hands like the others. She waited quietly, confident that the people who had rescued her would see her right.

She had many litters, the largest being 14 piglets and the smallest being just three. The first time she was due to farrow we watched with amusement as she made herself a 'nest'. She marched back and forth from her sty to the grass outside, grabbed a mouthful and marched back inside, grumbling to herself and - I could almost swear - casting very black looks in our direction as we sat on a bench at the end of an exhausting day in the tearoom, laughing at her. It was almost as if you could hear her saying: 'This is a fine mess you've got me into!'

A sow's gestation period is three months, three weeks and three days. In more profitable farms the sow is put back to the boar not long after weaning her piglets, as she comes into season almost straight away. This means that a sow can have up to three litters in just over a 12-month period. This is naturally exhausting for the sow and not the way we wanted to treat our Cassie. We always gave her a few months off, and this led to her being a happy, healthy pig who had happy, healthy piglets. We used to watch her playing with her piglets on occasion in the early days watching her run around in circles after them and reminding us that she was still a youngster herself.

The time she had just three piglets was a worrying day. Her average litters had been at least seven and we wondered why there were just three. We had heard that if a pig had trouble farrowing, the piglets left inside her would die and this could lead to infection. We called a vet, who examined her and declared that this was indeed the case, there were piglets stuck inside and injected Cassie with a drug that would bring on further contractions. If these were unsuccessful, the vet said we would have no other option but to shoot Cassie to stop further suffering*

She continued to shake with the contractions, but no more piglets emerged, so we phoned our ever-helpful neighbour Edward to come and suggest how we might best dispose of our lovely pig. "Bloody vet needs shooting," was Edward's diagnosis. He further explained that a pig's uterus is Y-shaped, and a small litter could be because only the eggs on one side of the uterus had been fertilised. A small litter was just that. A small litter. There was nothing wrong with Cassie, but as far as Edward was concerned there was a lot wrong with the vet.

To help her recover from what had been an unnecessarily prolonged labour, Edward brought her a bucket of milk. Foaming, frothy and full of fat and goodness, the bucket was from that morning's milking. Apparently, if a cow gets mastitis she still has to be milked, but the milk can't go into the food chain. Such was the bucket that Edward was carrying. Cassie lapped it up. She absolutely loved it, and it did her the power of good. She was up and back on her trotters in no time. I don't know how many of Edward's cows kept getting mastitis, but he had an awful lot of cows, and the frothy bucket of milk became a regular treat for our pigs after that first one. If they weren't able to wolf it all down in one go, (rare), the surplus was put into an old 40-gallon water butt and it would slowly turn into double cream, then yoghurt, both of which were also much appreciated. There is still some film festering away on a hardly seen Spillers Farm You Tube channel of Cassie and some of her piglets feasting on Edward's milk. The milk in turn softened their meat, meaning that we had the tastiest sausages and the most succulent liver for miles around.

Edward had once farmed pigs and I think he missed hanging around with them because following that incident he became a pretty regular visitor to Spillers, more often than not with a bucket of frothy milk in his hand. Or we would come home to find a brace of pheasant hanging by the back

door. It was Edward's calling card. He was an incredibly valuable resource. He had forgotten more about pigs than we would ever know and was full of help and advice. Before ringing the vet, we would always call Edward. One of our young sows got lice one day and as usual Farmer Edward had some interesting advice. He told us to put a stripe of engine oil down the middle of the pig's back. He told us that when the pig led down the lice would try to crawl to the other side and would drown in the oil. We did as he said and true enough the next day the pig was lice free.

After many happy years and many litters, eventually the day came when we knew Cassie was past her prime and we were going to have to let her go. We were not brave enough to take her to the slaughterhouse as we were too upset at the prospect, so once again the redoubtable Edward came to our aid. He offered to take her not to the slaughterhouse, but to the local livestock market, where people would go looking to purchase older animals not for human consumption. Cassie was - as she always was - minding her own business in one of the stalls when a woman walked past and said to Edward: "That's a nice-looking Saddleback. I've just got a Saddleback boar and she might make a nice companion. How much you selling her for?"

So once more Cassie became the death-defying pig and went off to a new life and a new boyfriend. Edward saw the woman again later at the market and heard that Cassie had had at least one more litter of piglets. Cassie must have been around nine years old at the time. When pigs are that age they are still capable of having piglets, but often the piglets can be small and runty or the litters can be small in number. Edward went to visit this woman and Cassie, and far from being small and runty she'd apparently had 13 lovely piglets and was very gentle when she led down for them to feed. She was a fabulously instinctive mother. I don't know what happened to her after that, but I somehow like to think she is plodding around a field to this day, quietly minding her own business.

*An interesting point to note here is that the vet was called out on an emergency call on a Sunday morning. He was with us for 90 minutes and injected Cassie. The whole thing cost £20. £20! For a vet's bill! Vets make their money from those animals with whom we are most emotionally involved. The vet knew we loved our dog and cats, he didn't realise how much we loved Cassie.

BRENDA AND THE CREAM TEA

The first few trips we took with Cassie to see her
boyfriend Rambo were pretty stressful. For a start
there was no sat nav then. Can you imagine? A
world without sat nav? I know, barbaric right?
Secondly, imagine you're in the countryside, so
there are no A roads, not even B roads sometimes.
Sometimes you're just driving down some track
with ruts, potholes and grass growing up the middle
of it. Thirdly, there aren't really many road signs.
There certainly aren't any road names, as there
aren't really any roads and - according to local
legend - all the directional signs were taken away in
the Second World War to confuse the Germans in
case they invaded, and nobody ever got round to
replacing them. Fourthly, you're trying to navigate
using an A-Z (ask your mum), an ordnance survey

map and instinct. Fifthly, you and your husband have no sense of direction between you and even though you did this trip a few months ago neither of you can really remember where you're going anyway, so the best thing to do is blame it on each other and shout names at each other above the noise that Brenda's making.

Brenda? Oh yes, Brenda. Brenda was a Land Rover Defender and (in the same manner as the purchase of our first proper trailer around the same time) signified another sign that we were becoming proper smallholders. Brenda was not a comfortable ride. She was a sort of tin can on wheels that was a nightmare to drive, leaky in the rain and freezing cold in the winter, but Brenda the Defender had become our vehicle. Great for towing trailers, really, really bad for a drive to Luton airport we once had to take to fly to a friend's 50th birthday party in Germany. (It took about seven noisy, bumpy, uncomfortable, unhappy hours - and the journey there wasn't easy either!).

One of the most amazing aspects of Brenda was the fact that she ran on leftover vegetable oil that we procured from a local chippie. We poured in the equivalent of a gallon of Crisp 'n' Dry and started her up. We only tried it once (not sure it's brilliant for the engine, might possibly be illegal), but it was a great magic trick.

The final straw with Cassie and the journeys to see
Rambo came after Cassie had obviously had
enough of being bumped about over the potholes in
a tin can on wheels. As I think I might have
mentioned, pigs are keen on food and so we used
to lure Cassie into the trailer with all sorts of her
favourite treats. Cabbage leaves and apples are
good * but like us, pigs are keen on the carbs, so
bread and cakes also go down well. So, there I
was in the back of the trailer - which had been
carefully filled with straw to make a lovely bed for
madam's journey - holding half a scone in one hand
which had been generously slathered with jam and
cream. That's right. Cassie was being offered her
own cream tea if she would only move one trotter
further forward and actually get in the trailer. She
had already eaten apples, cabbages and a possible
loaf and a half of bread in the three hours that I had
been cramped in the back of the trailer waiting for
her to move an inch or two further forwards. Three
hours people. Three hours! Did I mention that pigs
are clever? Well, Cassie had worked out that if she
moved that one trotter further forwards, she was
trapped, and Keith would be able to shut the door
on her capacious behind, that would be that and
we'd be off to see Rambo. And even though she
loved cream teas (who doesn't, to be fair), she
wasn't buying it.

At which point I gave in. I could bear it no longer.
She had won. I gave her the scone and crawled
out the trailer whilst I still had the use of my legs

and said to Keith as I wobbled past him the blood still not really making it to my feet, "We're getting a boar."

*I should mention here that pigs are most fond of the fruits and vegetables that accompany pork incredibly well. Which is sort of odd and I can't quite get the image of one of the piglets running around the yard outside their sty with an apple in its mouth, in all sorts of raptures of excitement. The trouble is, in my mind's eye I couldn't help but see the platter on which his head was sitting with the apple still firmly in place.

RODDERS, FARROWING AND 'STAY IN THE CAR MARLENE'....

I can't remember how we found Rodney Trotter or why somehow, we had ended up with Cassandra and Rodney before getting DelBoy and Raquel, but it seemed to suit them anyway.

But I think wherever we got Rodders from they were trying to get rid of him. He wasn't exactly a young boar in his prime. He was a bit of an older gentleman and, as far as I can remember on their first date, Cassie was rather keener on making bacon than he was. In fact, she was chasing (in a lumbering-ton-of-bricks-trying-to-run-sort-of-way) him round the yard whilst he was backing away with his crown jewels tucked underneath him, a panic-stricken 'you don't understand, I'm not that kind of pig' sort of look on his face.

At first, he lived in an outdoor sty on his own in the field. I'm sure you've seen them, as you've driven past a pig farm on the side of the motorway. From a distance they look like a lot of upturned corrugated tin cans. Great for summer housing, the portable pig sty is basically a big, corrugated tin hut with just about room for one large pig. Not enough room for one large pig and a human being, as Keith found to his consternation a day or two after Rodney arrived. He was on his hands and knees sorting out some lovely soft straw bedding for Rodders when he felt everything get a little cramped. Nudging Keith's backside and trying to settle himself into his newly made bed was Rodney. I should explain that Rodney was half the size of Cassie again, so he was at least six feet by four. (Attentive readers might stop at this point and ask themselves didn't she say Cassie was six by four? You're correct, I did. The fear of the pig equivalent of the Pamplona Bull Run made me exaggerate.) But with no exaggeration, Rodney was huge. He had the shoulders and neck of a porcine Prop Forward and he was now face to face with Keith in a twisted version of Goldilocks. Not really knowing Rodney or what he was capable of, Keith had nervously started to call out to me. I don't know why he was bothering. For a start, I was probably in the house making beds or cakes, and I don't know what he thought I was going to do about it. At the time I really didn't really like pigs and the last thing I was likely to do would be to beat Rodney's backside until he released his prisoner. I was more likely to let Rodney do what he liked with Keith and beg him to spare me for the sake of the hens.

But, as Keith crawled backwards out of the sty, quietly repeating "there's a good piggy, down piggy, good boy," to himself we were yet to realise just what a lovely gentle pig Rodney was. As we later learned, he was a real softie who loved a cuddle. If you tickled him under his expansive chin, he would grunt with pleasure and slowly sort of collapse and slide down a wall until he was lying on his side waiting for you to give him a belly rub. If you stopped, he would paw you with his trotter until you started again. Pigs are just dogs in disguise.

Rodney was doing his own version of glamping because we were in the middle of turning a Nissen Hut that was just behind the vegetable garden, into a first-class pig sty. I say we. I actually mean Edward. It was probably his idea. Once Edward heard we were going to start breeding (or rather, the pigs were), he pointed out that the Nissen Hut would make a fine sty and offered to convert it with the help of one of the lads that worked on his farm. Of course, we reckoned without Devonshire timing.

Things run a lot slower in the countryside. A lot slower. Not long after we moved into Spillers, I phoned the local cab firm on a Sunday to order a cab. "Arrh, if you'd wanted a cab on a Sunday, you need to have ordered it by Thursday at the latest," came the reply. Coming from pre-Uber Northwest

London where there were cab firms by the dozen with drivers just sitting around waiting for a fare any time day or night, this was an astounding reply. When we first arrived in the countryside there was still half-day closing on Wednesdays and Saturdays. There was a quaint charm about the pace of life in this new but old world we had come to inhabit. Not long after we moved in the postman rang our doorbell (only once). "Hello, I'm Nigel, your postie", he said. Fresh from London, I stood there staring at him slightly open-mouthed wondering if he was looking past me scouting the place to see if there was anything worth taking. No, nothing of the sort. He was Nigel, our local postie, just wanting to welcome us to the village. As we got used to this new and lovely way of life, we would leave the back door open whilst we took our dog for a walk. Often on our return we would find Nigel had been and left our post on the kitchen table. It was like reverse burglary. Something that I have now come to cherish, commercialism took second place to community, and building a Nissen Hut took as long as it took. It took 18 months.

The hut was divided by a large brick wall to provide two 'rooms'. It was a warm, safe and relatively large and comfortable accommodation for Rodney on one side and Cassie on the other, and the Trotter's Bottom sign hung proudly from the door. Now we had a sty worth of the name. Outside the hut was a relatively large concrete area for them to have some space during the winter when the field would be too muddy for their trotters, and beyond that a large portion of the lake field that we had fenced off using an electric fence. Well, it started as an electric fence. Due to their innate intelligence, pigs are very easy to train. Once they have had a belt from an electric fence, they don't forget it, and you can put up a piece of wire where the electric fence used to be, and they will not go near it.

We had three or four of these areas with different pig families in each. Marlene (our second breeding sow, a Gloucester Old Spot) with her piglets, Cassie with hers, Rodders (or our later addition DelBoy) with one or other of the girls or a visiting sow* all rooting around the field and grunting happily at each other. A very different life from the way in which most commercial pigs are raised – indoors on concrete with no access to space or light, in such terrible cramped conditions that the stress causes them to fight and truly damage each other. Sows are often put in a farrowing crate to give birth and feed their piglets. This awful contraption is a metal crate just big enough for the pig to lie in, but not move otherwise, not turn around or stand up. Pigs pay a terrible and high price for your bacon sarnie.

During the time of building, we kept putting Rodney and Cassie together (whenever we consulted the Pig Porn photos) and a few months later our first home-grown litter was born. Once the piglets arrived Rodney was duly sent back glamping.

Having a boar around piglets is not a good idea. Their instinct isn't particularly paternal.

Rodney was a Gloucester Old Spot and the combination of an Old Spot and a Saddleback produce a pig that is longer in the body and therefore makes a great bacon (imagine a combination of back bacon and streaky in one rasher), We also liked the fact that with one being a Gloucestershire pig and the other from the ancient now extant area of Wessex they were our local rare breeds and not just your run of the mill big, pink pig. They produced a range of glorious little piggies who were a combination of pink and black spots and stripes.

Nothing is quite as joyful as a litter of piglets (well, a group of orphan lambs gambolling around a field – more of which later – comes close). They are wonderful little creatures and tiny when born, particularly in comparison to their parents. They are almost instantly able to stand on their trotters, tiny perfect little pink things not unlike watching a ballerina en-pointe . Their skin has a soft, hairy down which looks almost furry and is so clean when they are born, for pigs are the cleanest of farm animals. They are great timewasters. Keith and I could stand for ages, just watching them play, nudging each other, play-biting each other's tails and faces, playing chase, grunting and squealing with pleasure, before all collapsing in a heap and snuggling into each other sleeping with soft grunts and snores, while mum just lies watching them play. It's not unlike watching a litter of puppies.

Pigs are fabulous at giving birth. Unlike their farmyard companions, sheep or to some extent cattle, they simply get on with it without any fuss and need absolutely no help from us, thank you very much. Quite often ours seemed to farrow (for that is the term not only for one half of an unnecessarily expensive tin of paint, but also for birthing pigs) at night and we would arrive at Trotters Bottom in the morning to see how they were getting on, only to find the whole thing had happened whilst we were asleep, mother having farrowed 10 piglets, cleaned them, the sty and herself and now they were all sleeping peacefully in the straw as if nothing had happened.

In fact, I was privileged to see a litter of piglets being born only once. We had probably been at Spillers for a few years, and I was happily watching a David Attenborough documentary one evening in March, when Keith popped his head around the door and said: "Do you want to see Marlene giving birth?" I looked from him to the TV, and realised I had my own wildlife documentary happening live a few hundred feet away and said: "Yeah, alright." as if it was the most natural thing in the world.

Natural and yet at the same time incredible. Unlike human birth it is a quiet experience. Marlene (as in 'Stay in the car, Marlene', Boyce's classic line in

Only Fools and Horses) was lying on her side breathing heavily. Every now and again her body would give a shudder and out would slip a piglet. Literally it just slid out. But here's the incredible bit. It was lying in the right direction to crawl its way round to her teats and immediately start suckling.

A regular sow will have 14 teats and can therefore easily feed a litter of 14, but as with many things in life it is a bit of a competition. The first piglet out crawls to the teats nearest the sow's head and latches onto a teat. The siblings that follow do the same, taking a top row or bottom row teat in turn until they are all taken. That will be its teat for the whole of the time it is feeding from her. There's no chopping and changing, that is its station. This all makes great sense. Pigs are born with their teeth and if there's a fight over a teat it could end in the teat being torn, injuring the mother and leaving a teat unusable and at least one piglet unfed. So, they all seem to know instinctively that they each have a feeding station and they stick to it. But here's the competition. The teats nearest the head contain a good deal of colostrum. Colostrum is the first form of milk produced by a mammal (including ourselves) after giving birth. It contains a whole bunch of good stuff and antibodies to guard against infection and produce vitality. The milk flow is stronger at the head, so those born first get the best milk and the one born last gets a weaker flow of milk. Poor little runts who get the least. But the joke is on those born first as they grow fastest and

– sadly – reach their slaughter weight first. Just as the one who laughs last laughs longest, the pig who is born last lives longest.

Whilst I'm droning on about how wonderful pigs are I must tell you another of my favourite things about them is their toilet habits. For some completely unfair reason pigs have a reputation for being dirty. We all seem to think that they are filthy, when nothing could be further from the truth. I think we get this idea because we see pigs rolling around in mud (and to be fair, they do do a lot of that for perfectly good reasons which I will explain at some point), but they are the cleanest animals in their own home. We get the idea that they are dirty from seeing them farmed commercially where they seem dirty and muddy. This is only because they do not have the space to defecate elsewhere. That is definitely not their choice. They are the only farm animals (certainly from the limited number of species we looked after) that don't poo in their own beds. Hens, ducks, sheep have no such qualms happily pooing and then lying down in it (sometimes the hens even tucking in when it had dried a bit), but you will never find a pig messing its own bed. The same piglets that I had seen born will within 24 hours have their first poo. And when they do, they get up from the straw where they are all snuggled on top of each other in a pyramid of pink and black spots and stripes and head off to the corner of the sty, where they do what is necessary and come back to bed and snuggle in. One is the bedroom, one is the en-suite and never the twain shall meet. They do this instinctively, nobody teaches them, it's just the way they are. Not for nothing were we (humans that is) once called Long Pigs in medieval times, (where long meant tall). We have a lot in common.

Once we had started breeding pigs, we seemingly couldn't stop. Cassie was soon joined by two further sows, Raquel and the previously mentioned Marlene. Both these girls were Gloucester Old Spots and unknown to us when she arrived Raquel was already pregnant. It wasn't long before she farrowed, and we had a bonus litter of piglets. Rodney coped well with his two new wives, and we set him up with Raquel again when the time was right. (As an Old Spot with a pink bottom it was easier to gauge when this was). She gave us a second litter of piglets, but this time tragedy struck. Being new to the game we had not realised the need for farrowing rails. Mummy Pig is big and heavy, and the piglets are small and sometimes mum can roll onto the piglets and crush them. Sadly, this is what happened to Raquel's second litter. She was young and inexperienced and so were we. She obviously didn't realise they were all so close to her. We came into the sty the morning after she had farrowed and found that she had crushed all 14 of her babies. It was the saddest sight. "Where you have livestock, you also have deadstock," Farmer Edward wisely told us later as he told us of the need for farrowing rails. These are rails that are situated along the walls of the sty. They are positioned so that they are low enough for the piglets to crawl underneath and escape from mum. Farrowing rails were immediately installed and we never lost another piglet.

*A visiting sow is a sow that comes to stay with the boar for a month whilst she is in season. Much like Cassie had gone to stay with Rambo. We had a number of visitors for both Rodney and DelBoy. Lucky them.

THE JOY OF PIGS

One thing that Long Pigs and Pig Pigs have in common is the expression of emotion, happiness and joy. Unless you've raised pigs that are truly free range and have plenty of room to roam, enough ground to root around with their snouts and chase a ball (yep, we bought toys for our pigs) you will not have seen a pig's 'happy face'. A pig's 'happy face' is a slightly open mouthed, joyful expression as if it is laughing (imagine Babe singing 'Jingle Bells' in the eponymous film and you're fairly close,) quite often seen whilst the pig is in full running mode chasing its siblings. They also enjoy a spa day. At least Marlene did. Marlene's spa treatment consisted of me rubbing her back with the head of an old yard broom, a sort of porcine exfoliation as it were, whilst she grunted with pleasure, before flopping down into a mud puddle for a good old bathe. It must be explained at this point that the reason pigs lie around in mud and generally almost cover themselves in it is due to their lack of sweat glands and their inability to sweat. They are a bit like Prince Andrew in that respect. And for those of you who think I have just compared Prince Andrew to a pig, I would say that is an insult to the pig. Therefore, when it's really hot, they like the mud to stop their skin burning (told you they were like us) and nobody has yet come up with a factor 100 sun protector product for pigs, so they opt for the mud. Many is the mud bath that I gladly made for Marlene and her piglets to splash and play in during the summer months. Many is the time that I got splattered as she decided to have a shake and helpfully cover me too.

So pet-like were they for us in fact, that we once took Cassie on a walk. Our largest field backed onto that our of our neighbour and within a few hundred yards to the right of that field was a footpath/lane called Dead Horse Lane. (Best not to dwell on why). Dead Horse Lane was lined with oak trees on either side and during the autumn it was covered with acorns. Literally covered. On discovering that pigs are naturally wood-inhabiting creatures who love acorns - in medieval times pigs were fattened on acorns prior to slaughter- we took

Cassie for a walk down Dead Horse Lane and she loved it. She snuffled along, munching acorns for all she was worth. Pigs, by the way, not only love acorns; they also love weeds. Whenever I had any spare time I was weeding. We had 14 acres of land and weeds never stop growing. After I had filled a bucket with weeds, I would tip it over the fence to the pigs who would grunt their thanks and immediately start rooting around to find their favourite bit – bindweed. there must be something about the taste of bindweed because every pig munched on that first.

Maybe because they love weeds so much, pigs are also great gardeners. Well, perhaps that is stretching a metaphor a little too far. What they are good at is rooting around in soil, pushing it up with their snouts to look for food. The pig's snout is incredible. The very tip of it is incredibly sensitive, can pick up smells from miles around. It is also flexible and soft, so that the pig can gently snuffle your hand to see what treat you may be offering. But behind that soft end is a hard bit of cartilage which is strong enough to push up concrete if time allows. If you want to turn over a piece of ground and get all the roots out and the rocks and stones to the top for easy removal, get a pig to do it. They are like rotavators, rotavators you have to feed and house, but they are worth it. Give them a patch of ground and some time and without you having to lift a finger, they will have eaten the grass, turned over the soil, taken out all the roots and fertilised it to boot. Then you bring in the hens. The hens will do the fine weeding, scratching small patches of ground to look for insects and eating the weeds as they go. They are a great team, and before you know it, they will have turned a rotten patch of ground into a fine tilth. And so, you and your husband now have no choice but to plant at least seven enormous vegetable beds, and try to make yourselves self-sufficient and turn in to Tom and Barbara from The Good Life.

THE GOOD LIFE

The 'Good Life' is what everyone dreams about. This is the fantasy that many who came to stay at Spillers wanted to make their own. The dream that you can raise your own meat, grow your own veg, and still have the energy to actually cook it and eat it without falling asleep in the middle of dinner. Because it is the most exhausting, energy sapping lifestyle I have ever had the privilege to experience.

But we pretty much did it. We turned part of the lake field into a very large vegetable garden with seven large (think the size of one allotment) veg beds. These veg beds were created using telegraph poles as borders. Not cut up into pieces, but the whole telegraph pole. That gives you some idea of the size. Keith grew most of the veg from seed and we grew a lot. One bed contained just onions. Trying to be fairly organic we fertilised everything with liquid pig poo. Basically, you put it in a water butt and let the rain do the rest. To fertilise the veg plots you scoop it out in a bucket and throw it all over the ground. It was marvellous stuff and meant that some of our veg was enormous. It was also very much needed. The soil in our part of East Devon was very heavy clay. It was such heavy clay you could have made a plate from what was left on your spade from your first dig. It stuck to your boots like glue making it hard to lift your feet as you trudged back from the fields.

We might have had to eat a lot of cabbage one spring to do it, but by the end of our time at Spillers we were self-sufficient in our fruit and veg. If we didn't grow it, we didn't eat it. Ironically, spring was the leanest, hardest time. The vegetables from the previous year have pretty much been eaten and although the new veg has been planted, it's not really producing anything much yet. We had lots of apples stored at the end of autumn, but by the spring many of them had turned because of the blemishes on them. The pigs were delighted with this turn of events. Spring is when the self-sufficient smallholder eats a lot of pickles, blemished apples and whatever is left in the freezer. Usually cabbage.

Pigs can be slaughtered at any time of the year

(their destiny depending on how much weight they have gained until they reach 'slaughter weight'. We worked this out by measuring their bellies to determine how heavy they were), but – despite their association with spring – lambs are not ready to slaughter until the autumn. I used to think that when we ate lamb it was the tiny, little, creature boinging round the field that had just been born. But they are much, much bigger and fatter than that by the time they go. We associate lamb and spring because of our historic reliance on New Zealand lamb (which would be imported here during their autumn and our spring), so our meat choices became quite limited in the spring. I made brawn one year. Only once. It lasted fand, in the end,the end even Merryck was sick of eating it.

Sadly, we failed in the dairy department, although we dabbled with the idea of getting goats, (Keith having kept them in a previous attempt to kill himself through exhaustion in his thirties) but with the Bed and Breakfast (don't worry, we'll come to that) and holiday cottage (that also) side of things, we simply didn't have the time.

We tried hard though. Market days were the busiest, when Keith would bring back the meat from the local abattoir – a small, family-run establishment a couple of miles away. The sausages would arrive in one incredibly long string of about 400 and we would spend a couple of hours cutting them into smaller sections and bagging

them for the freezer. 1,2,3,4,5,6, cut, bag.
1,2,3,4,5,6, cut, bag. Then Keith would make bacon
- basically taking the whole side of the pig and
salting it on both sides, then placing it in a large
plastic container and leaving it. After 24 hours the
water would be drained off and it would be re-salted
and replaced. This would continue for a month and
then, lo and behold, you have bacon.

Living the self-sufficient lifestyle we wanted to
honour the animal who had given its life to enable
us to live ours and so we wasted nothing. When it
came to the pigs we tried to eat everything but the
oink. We tried to eat tongue once. Keith's brother
had come to stay for the night with a friend. They
were keen to stay for dinner, until I told them dinner
was Tongue with Caper sauce. For some reason,
they went out to the local pub. To be honest that
was the only time we tried to eat tongue. It's a bit
like kissing the pig and something you should only
attempt if you're really starving, or French. But,
after that first attempt at total pig consumption, we
did roast the heads, tails and trotters for our dog.
The first head I roasted it felt utterly macabre.,
opening the oven door to find I was being looked at.
But we got used to it and Merryck loved a bit of
pig's head, especially the ears – a porky lug as we
called them. We would roast a head for hours in the
AGA, then strip off the meat and mix it with rice. It
would feed him for weeks.

We grew a great many vegetables and bought a

very large polytunnel which housed 40 tomato plants. We planted apple trees, plum trees, and lots of soft fruit canes including raspberry, tayberry, loganberry (all pretty much the same if you ask me). As well as bacon and sausages, we made ham, chorizo and even once attempted to make our own hay by scything a patch of long grass with a pair of hand scythes I found in the garage which made us look like a cross between the Amish and the Grim Reaper. Keith built a smoker out of an old oil drum, and we cold smoked mackerel fished from the sea at Lyme Regis. We foraged a lot. I picked blackberries, crab apples and scoured the hedges along our fields to find a few hazelnuts. I became an expert pickler and chutney maker. Keith made the jam. Two roles we still fulfil to this day. I even subjected the tearoom customers to nettle soup and a dandelion leaf salad, which one long-suffering customer derided saying she had eaten better. Whether or not she meant she had eaten a better dandelion leaf salad or had eaten better generally I did not wish to discover.

We bought an incubator and hatched both duck and hen eggs to increase our flock of both, which was a fascinating thing to do. The incubator is set at a warm temperature, and eggs are put inside. You have to turn the eggs every day and after a few days you use a process called candling (by holding the egg up to the light of a candle) to see if there's an embryo growing inside. The whole process takes about a month. As the eggs get ready to hatch, they start to chirp to each other. The chicks inside are communicating with the rest of the brood to come out. Then one egg will start to crack. To aid its journey, the chick has an Egg Tooth, a small, sharp horn-like growth which is used to help crack the shell. It takes a few hours, but the chick will chip away from the inside until it has made a large enough crack and eventually it will emerge, shaking the rest of the shell from its wet, slightly feathery body, looking for all the world like a tiny little dinosaur. It will be another few hours before it dries off, fluffs up and looks like the cute thing on top of a supermarket chocolate Easter cake.

We also had hens that went broody on their own and hatched their own chicks all on their own without any help from us too. Trying to get the eggs out from under a broody hen is a brave thing to do. A broody or a mother hen is a fearless and quite fearsome creature. She will take on anyone and anything to save her eggs or chicks. You try to get an egg out from under a broody hen and you can expect to be pinned with a very fierce beady eye and get a very sharp peck for your trouble. Hens make the most brilliant mothers though. Once they have had their brood they protect them with their lives, and it is a joy to see the mother hen spread her wings to keep her little ones dry in the rain (the actual physical example of being taken under someone's wing) or even watch them climb into her feathers, and see a little head peeking out;

it's a wonderful thing. They also teach them to eat, dropping crumbs in front of them until they get the idea for themselves.

Strangely, ducks don't have the Egg Tooth, which seems unfair. Their beaks are softer, rounder and their shells are much harder, so the whole process is much more arduous for them. With our first brood of ducklings, we made the mistake of 'helping' the first little duckling out of its shell, by picking it off them. The poor little thing died within a few hours of hatching. The process of fighting their own way out of the shell is obviously necessary for giving them the strength for life and our 'helping' didn't help at all.

It's all very well bringing these little creatures into the world, but once you've done it you have to act like their parents and teach them about everything including the lake. How do you get them there? That's another story.

A CAPTAIN GOES DOWN WITH HIS SHIP

One of the loveliest things about Spillers was the lake. We called it a lake, although one Trip Advisor reviewer called it a large pond, a description that Keith found particularly hard to forgive, although seeing as she was from America – land of the Great Lakes – she probably had a different perspective on it than us. As Keith was regularly heard to exclaim after this review, "Swans nest on it. That ballet's not called Swan Pond, is it?!"

Pond or lake, the patch of water in our big field was a joy. Swans did indeed nest there and raise cygnets year after year (with varying degrees of disaster, more of which later), and it was a regular haunt of herons, moorhens, coots, egrets and the very occasional kingfisher. Unfortunately, it was also the haunt of what became our nemesis, the cormorant. A master fish catcher, the cormorant is a protected species, which is a shame, because they nearly emptied our lake of fish with their almost constant presence. In the summer, many gorgeously coloured dragonflies flew around us trying to dodge the swooping swifts that would catch them and other insects on the wing as we pootled around the lake in our rowing boat looking at the water boatmen flitting around on the top of the water.

Our little boat with its mismatched oars (one long, one short, a bit like Keith and I) was a great source of entertainment for us and our dog Merryck as we used to race him from the shore to the island. The lake had been created by the previous owners of Spillers by basically digging a big hole in the field and piling up the excavated soil into a mound in the middle. This created the island. As the water table around Spillers was so low, water filled in the big ditch around the island, and that basically created the lake. It was fed by natural springs, so there was a constant flow of clear, clean water. When we arrived, the lake had only been in existence for a couple of years and did look a bit like a hole in the ground filled with water. Over the 10 years of our occupancy, we planted quite a few things around the lake, some water irises, some hostas, some gunneras, but we didn't really plant any trees. The trees just arrived somehow. By the time we left

Spillers, the lake and the island had been transformed. There were willows all around it and it was beautiful. Willow seeds only germinate if they fall on wet soil and there was plenty of that around the lake. The seeds would have come from fluffy catkins borne on the wind from some other nearby White Willows, (there were plenty on the banks of the River Axe which flowed at the bottom of Farmer Edward's field which backed onto our land), and over the ten years of our time at Spillers many, many seeds turned into plenty of lovely willows edging the lake. Rushes had also sprung up and colonies of waterlilies grew in large patches around the edges. It was a real lesson in how beautiful nature is if you just let it do its thing.

We had names for various parts of the lake. Keith and I have a ridiculous habit of naming things - as you may have gathered from us calling one of our cars Brenda. We named one of our fridges Sheila as there was a LED display on the door of her temperature of three degrees. (You might need someone old to explain the correlation between Sheila and The Three Degrees. Someone old. Or Google). One corner of the lake was soft and gently framed with waterlilies and willows, we called it Virginia Water after the genteel Surrey countryside. Opposite to that was the Corner with No Name, and adjacent to that was Bottomy Bay where the outflow of the septic tank fed into the lake. The outflow of the septic tank was cleaned through a reed bed system, which ensured that by the time it

got to the lake it was sparkling and clean water –
despite the name we gave it!

The lake was a place of many things. We swam in
it, we rowed on it, and we even walked on it one
year when it froze for over a month and the ice was
at least a foot deep. I even fell in it once when I
overbalanced trying to fill up a watering can. We
should have filmed it for You've Been Framed, but
the phone was still in my pocket. We put benches
and tables around it for us and the guests to enjoy
its gentle beauty. And this made it a place of quiet
contemplation. We had a group of friends often
come and swim in it and this made it a place of fun.
We rowed our boat and played a game of 'Splash
Water' with our dog Merryck who would swim
beside us whilst we tried to splash him. But before
any of that really happened it was the scene of an
almost Titanic-like disaster where Keith nearly went
down with the ship.

We had taken our newly hatched ducklings to the
lake one morning when we knew they would be
waterproof. Ducklings that are naturally hatched
are made waterproof by their mother's grooming.
She releases something into their feathers which
makes them buoyant. If they have been hatched
artificially this waterproofing process will happen
naturally, but it takes three weeks. So, after 21
days or so, we took them to the lake, released them
at the edge and watched them happily paddle away
from us. Ahh, we felt such pride.

All that pride would come crashing down as we tried to get them to come home. The older ducks came waddling back as daylight began to fall as they did every day, but the ducklings weren't with them. Fearing the arrival of Mr Fox, we set off for the lake to bring our babies home. Our babies weren't the slightest bit interested in coming home. They were all happily installed on the lake preening themselves and ignoring us. This was in our very first year and our boat at that time was a blow-up dinghy, we had not yet got around to buying the aforementioned Lookfar with its peeling paint and mismatched oars. Our vessel was one of those dinghies you get at the seaside to give your kids a bit of fun for an afternoon. Keith set off to collect the ducklings whilst I was left on the shore to guide them home when they reached me.

Them reaching me turned out to be quite a palaver. Having managed to shoo them off the island, Keith paddled after them for all he was worth. Four little ducklings can be a terror to herd. Whichever way he paddled, they turned as one in the opposite direction. I was running up and down the shore with my arms outstretched desperately trying to get them to land, but as soon as they got close, they took fright and off they went into the middle of the water again, for the whole farce to start over. Keith paddling, them darting in the opposite direction, Keith shouting that I should be going in the other direction, them getting close, then off they'd go to the middle of the water, and we'd all start again.

By now, our shenanigans had raised the interest of several of our caravanning guests. There was a small Caravan Club CL site adjacent to the lake and alerted by our shouts that something of interest might be happening, they started to line up along the fence, drinks in hand, to watch. I think some of them might even have dragged their chairs along and really settled down.

So, not only were we making a complete hash of getting our dear ducklings home, but we also now had an audience. I am only grateful there was no TikTok, or it might still be a meme to this day. After half an hour I was not only knackered, humiliated and contemplating divorce but I was prepared to let the fox have the damn ducks when Keith started shouting with even more urgency: "I'm going down, Bridge, I'm going down!" I'm sure I heard ripples of laughter from the fence line as I looked to see the back half of the boat was definitely in the water. Our trusty vessel had sprung a leak, and Keith and the boat limped across the water to join me on the shore. We tried to pump it up with the foot pump to no avail, and so I tried to blow it up manually. After nearly giving myself a reverse panic attack with the hyperventilation needed to try and manually inflate a dinghy and hearing the - by now I was sure - gales of laughter from the vanners we decided to call it a day and if the fox got the ducklings, well, so be it. We'd had enough.

The next day dawned bright and clear, and it was with some apprehension we followed the ducks up the lake expecting to see fluffy little bodies littering the shoreline. But no such disaster had occurred. There were the ducklings, happy as Larry, all preening themselves on the island. I think they had the sense to stay overnight on the island and this had probably saved them from the fox. They quackily slipped into the water and joined their compatriots. Did we try to get them back the next night? No, we did not. And it seemed we didn't have to, for they did what nature would probably have instinctively made them do the night before if we hadn't got in the way. They just followed the other ducks home like it was the most natural thing in the world.

A SHEEP THAT WAS FLUFFY AND ONE THAT SWAM

"There's a sheep on the island." I put the tea tray down on the table where there sat two tearoom customers and gave the speaker a steady gaze. "What?" "There's a sheep on the island," the speaker repeated. "What, one of our sheep?" "Well, yes, I suppose so", she continued. "We just let the dogs run in the field, we didn't know there were sheep in it, and she must've got scared. She jumped into the lake and swam to the island."

There are two things to learn from this story. Firstly, don't let your dog run off the lead in a field until you're sure there are no sheep in it. And secondly, don't try to get a scared, soaking wet sheep off an island and into a boat. The first is common sense, the second makes no sense. But it does provide another story of hilarity involving Keith, the lake and a boat.

We had probably been at Spillers for a year or two at this point. We had pigs, ducks and we may well have had hens (more of which later). The next animal we had decided to take on were orphan lambs. Orphan lambs are so called sometimes because the ewe dies whilst lambing making her lambs true orphans, or she may have too many lambs to cope with. Unlike pigs and their 14 teats, ewes are a bit like us girls with a more modest two - one on each side. Two lambs are therefore ideal, but she may birth three or four resulting in not enough milk for them all. The solution is often to take the extra lambs and hand feed them. Naturally affectionate creatures, hand-reared lambs are the most adorable little things, prone to follow their feeder wherever he or she may roam, like Mary's little lamb of the nursery rhyme. And if you happen to have a large, very white Golden Retriever who is roughly the same size as a fully-grown sheep, you'll find the lambs will think he's their mum and not only will they follow him too, but they will also head-butt his belly to see if it will provide dinner. It won't, but he'll let you do it anyway, because he's a big softie.

So, one spring morning we tootled off in Brenda to a farm near Lyme Regis to pick up four orphan lambs. We decided that we would hand-rear them, then put them to a ram the following autumn and create our own little flock. On arrival it was fascinating to see the whole lambing process in operation. The farmer led us into his very large barn which was divided up into pens full of straw which gave the whole barn a wonderful, sweet aroma mixed with a musty, woolly sort of smell like damp pullovers. Some ewes had birthed and were lying with their lambs on the straw, some were in labour and there were several orphan lambs in their own little pens. Like a maternity ward, it was incredibly noisy - there was a lot of bleating. I have such respect for farmers, particularly around lambing time. Like us, sheep can give birth at any time of the day or night, so lambing is a 24 hour a day process involving the whole farming family taking it in turns to do day and night shifts. Unlike pigs, sheep are absolutely hopeless at giving birth. They need to be watched constantly. Sheep can be quite fearful creatures and I have heard of a sheep giving birth, getting a bit freaked out by the whole thing and just running off leaving the defenceless lamb to sort itself out. So, having orphan lambs is just one more thing the farmers have to deal with, and they are usually quite happy to offload some of the orphans onto unsuspecting smallholders.

Bryan, our lambing, farming guy reached into one of the pens, picked up one of the orphans by its forelegs and handed it to me. Over the years I learned that you pick up a lamb by its forelegs, but a piglet by its hindlegs and hold it upside down. One of the reasons may be something to do with volume. A lamb will lie still quite happily and silently let you carry it where're you wish. A piglet will struggle and fight to get free and squeal as if you are killing it and keep that screaming, squealing up at ear-splitting decibels until you put it down again. You don't want that end of the piglet too near your ears. It's deafening.

Keith had also gained a lamb, so we headed out and put them in the back of Brenda and fetched a couple more. They bleated a bit on the 20-minute drive back to Spillers but seemed quite at home in the back of the Land Rover and I remember looking at them and thinking in wonder at how much my urban existence in London had disappeared. The back of my car used to be full of shopping bags. Now it was full of woolly jumpers of a different kind. And here's the strangest part of that whole experience. There was a distinct odour in the car. The lambs smelt of something, a familiar scent that I couldn't quite place. Then it came to me. I turned to Keith and said: "Do you know what I can smell?" "Roast lamb."

The next few weeks were a little like having newborns, in that the lambs needed to be bottle fed four times a day and it was all a blur of making up the formula (which smelt incredibly sweet), feeding them, washing and sterilising the bottles and then before-you-know-it you're starting that process all over again. Over the years, we had many orphan lambs and bottle feeding them was always incredibly popular with friends, B&B guests and tearoom customers. Strangely enough though it was always Keith and I on the six am shift, shushing the lambs who were bleating loudly and running around our legs desperate to get some breakfast. In the field the lambs will take a little bit of milk from mum, a little bit of grass, so on and so forth throughout the day. A bottle-fed lamb will take as much milk as you will give it in one go. Sheep can be greedy creatures, (can't we all?) and the lambs would go nuts for the bottled milk gulping it down as quickly as they could and then lying around with enormous bellies in a sort of milk-induced 'coma'. Whilst they're gulping down the sweet milk their tails wag furiously back and forth, incredibly fast. "I'll be back in two shakes of a lamb's tail," means you'll be back incredibly quickly. When they first arrive, the tails are quite long, with a small rubber band halfway up the tail. This band has been put there to cut off the circulation to the rest of the tail, so that in time it drops (or is rather, wagged) off. It sounds cruel but the alternative is worse. For as the sheep poos, it lifts up its now-much-smaller tail to allow the poo to drop. If the tail was still long, it would obstruct this action and flies would gather and lay their eggs there enabling the maggots to eat the sheep from the inside out. Flystrike is still something for which lambs and sheep have to be treated even with the tail docking.

I'm sure it's quite painless, and the same method is used to remove the testicles of the male lambs. We had a couple of orphan lambs that were male once. We bought a contraption to do the tails and the boy bits. It's like a cross between a pair of scissors and eyelash curlers. You put a small rubber ring across the the top, close the handles which opens the band up, insert the tail, or the bits and SNAP it shut. Just lost all the male readers there.

Eventually, we realised you could buy a holder for the bottles rather than having to do it by hand, and we would set the bottles in the holder and have races to see which lamb finished first. If you care to look, there is still a video on Spillers Farm You Tube Channel from 2013 filming one of these races, which I am amazed to say has (at the time of writing) had 47,000 views. If you do bother to go and look it up, please bear in mind this was filmed a long time before TikTok made everyone a professional film director and Andrew Cotter had made animal eating competitions a viral You Tube sensation. It was also obviously a very windy day.

We had lots of orphan lambs over the years, and they are such joyful creatures. I defy anyone not to smile, grin or even through your head back and belly laugh at the antics of gambolling lambs running round a field. It truly lifts the spirits to see them springing on all fours in a movement which can only be described as 'boinging' and chasing each other about just for the sheer joy of running. To me that sight is the essence of spring. But no lambs were quite like our first, particularly the two we kept. At the end of the summer, we took two lambs to slaughter and two we didn't. They would be the ones to start our flock.

One of them was an incredibly pretty and incredibly fluffy lamb who, as she grew into sheephood, gained the name Pretty Fluffy Sheep, shortened to PFS which then got shortened to PF. (Occasionally, I called her Edith for my own amusement). The other was possibly the ugliest sheep you've ever seen. So, we called her Gollum.

And it was now Gollum who had taken fright and decided to become the world's first swimming sheep. I had no idea that sheep could swim. But if there is one thing that I learned during my time at Spillers it is not to underestimate any animal. Even one of our cats went for a swim in the lake. But that's another story.

So, Keith is back on the lake on another foolhardy mission. As per usual in these situations my position is supervisory, shouting encouragement from the shore. He reached the island and encountered his first problem. Catching Gols (her name also got shortened.) She did not want to be caught. She'd been frightened enough thank you. She was not crossing the sea again. She was happy to be an islander for the rest of her life.

After chasing Gols around for a while, somehow, he managed to grab hold of her and then he encountered his second problem.   Getting Gols in the boat. Do you remember woollen swimming trunks? To readers of a certain age they may be quite familiar. To younger readers born in an age of lycra they may seem quite ridiculous. And they were ridiculous. But trust me, such a thing did exist. Quite how anyone ever conceived of wool as a buoyancy aid is beyond me. Wool soaks up and retains liquid to an incredible degree. And it becomes incredibly heavy. And sheep are covered in wool, the world's most impractical swimming material. So, Keith is now manhandling a very wet, very heavy, very frightened sheep who wants to live on the island and certainly doesn't want to get into a boat. Sheep are not good sailors. The owl and the pussycat went to sea (there's those mythical water-loving cats again) not the owl and the sheep, and Gols is not going to get into some sea-faring craft any time soon, thank you very much.

Meanwhile, I'm shouting encouragement from the shore and watching our water-loving dog Merryck have the time of his life swimming to the island, running around with Keith and Gols and generally thinking this is a great afternoon's sport. Fortunately, we didn't have any caravanners in or they'd have been uploading this to You've Been Framed and getting their second payments of £250.

And with that, Gols decides she's had enough of being chased about and throws herself back into the water and starts to swim to shore. Imagine wearing the heaviest, woolliest swimming suit you can find, get it soaking wet, and start swimming, then let it dry out for 10 minutes and start swimming again. You'd probably find it really hard work and start to sink. And this is what began happening to our lovely, ugly sheep. Keith rushed to launch the boat, jumped in and started paddling towards her to help her out. Every time he got near, she'd swim in the other direction and so it continued for a few heart-stopping minutes, until Gols made it back to shore. She dragged her heavy, woollen body up the bank and carried on eating grass as if nothing had happened.

You would think that was the most remarkable thing about Gols, but she had another surprise for us a bit later on. But before that, I must tell you about PF.

PF

PF was the most adorable creature in the world. The most affectionate sheep anyone has ever known, she would stop eating for a cuddle and an ear scratch. And seeing that PF was also probably the greediest creature in the world that's quite something. That's her and me on the front cover and you can tell from our expressions it's mutual love.

There was just something about PF. Maybe it was her fluffiness, maybe it was the expression on her face when having a cuddle or an ear scratch, but she was a unique and lovely sheep. Maybe it was the fact that she'd been found wandering around the lake field with an iron ornament impaled through her cheek. A couple of our friends had visited from London and had bought us an iron bottle and wine glass holder made by a local blacksmith at nearby Branscombe forge. A lovely gift that we put on the lake shore by a bench with the intention of using it for an after-work tipple - if we ever stopped working. The top of it resembled a shepherd's crook. Maybe it was something instinctive that made PF want to go near a shepherd's crook – who knows – but within a week of it being there, she'd managed to get it stuck through her cheek and impaled herself upon it.

Because if there's another thing I learned about the difference between sheep and pigs it's this. Sheep are stupid and have a death wish. Keith always said about lambs and sheep that he'd never known anything so cute turn into something so ugly so quickly. And they are stupid. If a pig is stuck in a situation, they look for a way out. They are immensely intelligent creatures. If you're ever in a shipwreck with pigs by the way, follow the pig, because they instinctively swim towards the nearest shore. Sheep are the antithesis. If they are stuck in a situation, they just give up and die. I removed the crook from her face and treated the wound with Germolene – which seemed to do the trick. Maybe it was this that bonded us. Who knows, but PF and I were in love.

She knew her name and would come to it like a dog. This was even more remarkable when she joined our friend's flock of four hundred sheep in the field next to Spillers. Aiming to start our own flock, we put Gols and PF in with these four hundred sheep in the autumn and winter after we got them, just to see what would happen. When I was missing my girls, I would walk into their field and shout "PF, PF, PF" at the crowd of four hundred fluffy bodies. From the middle of the bodies would come a stirring, then a distinct movement as two sheep pushed their way to the edges of the group and PF would come charging towards me, closely followed by her ugly sister. We would throw ourselves at each other and I would bury my hands and face into her substantial and soft fleece.

I loved that sheep.

We hoped that during their winter sojourn in our neighbours' field they would get to know our neighbours' ram well enough to do the dirty and get themselves pregnant. They came back after a few months and continued their lives as wandering lawn mowers. Since Gols' attempt to become the ovine Sharron Davies, they were no longer safe in the lake field, so we had moved them to another couple of smaller adjacent fields. To ensure that no other animals went wild swimming Keith built a fence around the lake one weekend whilst I was visiting my sister. He took everything up there plank, by plank by hand. It was a pretty big stretch of water and was an impressive job. That man was born to be a smallholder. Jack of all trades, master of absolutely none.

The sheep stayed in our two side fields for a few weeks, meaning we didn't see them every day, so it came as a great surprise one morning when I went to check on them and what did I see peeking out from behind Gollum's back as she lay ruminating but her own little lamb! Despite everything I have just told you about sheep and their ineptitude for birthing, Gollum had just gone and done it on her own. Scared and timid she may have been, but there was the cutest little thing (with the biggest ears) hiding behind her mum. No mess, no fuss, Gollum must've given birth in the middle of the night, cleaned it all up and took it all in her stride. We instantly christened the lamb Precious, which will make some sense to those who are familiar with The Lord of the Rings trilogy. Precious was the cutest little thing. Just like many newborn lambs she looked like she'd been put into a pullover that was too big, her fleece was all wrinkly like Nora Batty's stockings (ask your Gran). We impatiently waited for PF to do the same, but no other lambs were forthcoming. In the commercial farming world if a sheep doesn't lamb in her first year of life she goes to slaughter. There is no point, profit or sense in keeping a barren sheep. But we were not commercial farmers and besides, I loved that sheep. So, we decided to give her another go.

Enter Mr Darcy.

Mr Darcy was a Wiltshire Horn. Another rare breed animal from vaguely the right area of the country to be local, Mr Darcy's speciality was the ability shed his own fleece. This wasn't particular to Mr Darcy, but it is particular to the Wiltshire Horn breed. Our thinking went that if we could breed our sheep with Mr Darcy, they too would be self-shedding and eliminate the need to bother Bryan (our lambing, farming guy) by asking him to sheer our tiny little flock whilst he's busy sheering his hundreds.

I was pretty wary of Mr Darcy. Merryck our lovely Golden Retriever (who will soon have his own chapter) was downright terrified of him and was very grateful for the five-bar gate that separated Mr Darcy from the rest of the world.

PF wasn't that keen on Mr Darcy either. He tried it on with both her and Gollum and got a nip on the ankles from Gollum for his trouble. He couldn't get anywhere near them. Every time he tried, Gollum would put herself between him and PF as if she was defending PF's honour. It makes me wonder if PF was more into ewes than rams but only Gollum had worked this out.

THE SOAY, OR BEWARE OF FREE GIFTS

"Look at this, this flock of sheep are being given away", Keith was reading from our new favourite read, the newsletter for the Devon Association of Smallholders or DASH for short. Never ones to turn down a bargain, we were keen to take them on. Besides, getting a free flock was a lot quicker than waiting for the daily ankle-nipping contest in our fields to turn into something more productive. So, we called the number for the free sheep and were told they would be delivered to us that weekend.

The flock in question were a group of Soay. According to Wikipedia, "the Soay sheep is a breed of domestic sheep (Ovis aries) descended from a population of feral sheep on the 100-hectare island of Soay." Well, our little flock of 14 Soay hadn't descended very far. They were almost completely feral, incredibly flighty and impossible to control. This is obviously why they were delivered to us free of charge, after darkness had fallen one January Sunday afternoon, offloaded into one of our side fields with the previous 'owners' beating a hasty retreat and very likely breathing an enormous sigh of relief.

In complete contrast to our lovely, tame sheep Gols and PF, who would surge towards us at the sound of our voices for cuddles and a chat, the Soay, (quite small and very light creatures, brown and with little horns – useful for handling if you could ever catch one) would flee from us at the sight of our approach as one, and leap Gazelle-like the hedge boundary between our side fields and cower nervously in the corner, ready to flee again at a moment's notice. The idea of getting hold of them to check their hooves, shear them or for any other husbandry purpose was completely out of the question. Little wonder they had been offered free of charge.

Wikipedia further adds that "the Soay is much smaller than modern domesticated sheep but hardier, and is extraordinarily agile (and then some), tending to take refuge amongst the cliffs when frightened." How I wish Wikipedia had existed then. It would have saved us much trouble.

However, in our blissful ignorance, we decided to let Mr Darcy have his day and led him into the field to see if he could take charge. After much fleeing and chasing, they all seemed to settle down for a few weeks, but we realised that in the long run the Soay would always be a complete nightmare.

And so, we once again were saved by our redoubtable neighbour Edward. One day we found him leaning on our five-bar gate watching Darcy chase the Soay around and - skilfully hiding his amusement at our idiocy in taking them on – offered to take them to market for us. It took four experienced sheepdogs, two quadbikes, six people and four hours to get 14 Soay into the back of a trailer. As per usual, my part in the proceedings was supervisory. This time from miles away, watching the shenanigans from the kitchen, pretending I had nothing to do with any of it.

But the fun doesn't end there. On arrival at Shepton Mallet market, Edward suggested they be put in a pen with extra high sides – the ones usually reserved for bulls. But nothing seemed to be high enough for our Soay, for once unloaded they did their usual and took flight. Leaping and jumping in all directions they had soon cleared the pen and were heading for the exits. The alarm bells went off and the main shutters for the whole market were closing; hopefully they would shut before the Soay made it to Shepton Mallet High Street. Meanwhile, farmers, market workers and spectators were all making a grab for the passing Soay. Somehow, they were all captured and returned to the pen and the chaos died down.

Edward proved to be our lucky charm at that market, for a woman passing the pen took a liking to the flock and bought them for her rare breed petting zoo. We heard in later weeks that Mr Darcy had managed to seduce some of them into standing still for a minute or two at least, as a few of them had given birth to tiny little Soay/Darcies; cute little, brown lambs with horns. Cute, as long as they were in someone else's field!

Sadly, one day soon after that we found Darcy dead in a field. It happens. As Edward would often say, "Where you have livestock, you also have deadstock." And the dream of our own little flock died with him.

So, what were we to do with Gols and PF now?

PFR AND THE COMPASSIONATE CARNIVORES

We gave them another summer. After all, Gollum had given us one lamb so we knew she could do it, and I was still hopeful that PF would come through. But sadly, neither of them produced anything further for us. And so came the difficult decision that every true smallholder must face.

I had coined the phrase 'Compassionate Carnivores' to describe how Keith and I viewed meat. "Oh, I couldn't eat an animal that I'd met" was a phrase we often heard from B&B guests when they complimented us on our delicious sausages and home-produced bacon. I would counter that I couldn't eat one that I hadn't. After all, we saw what went into them and that, in turn, would go into us. With supermarket meat, you've basically got no idea. We had very high husbandry standards. We loved our animals, they were well fed, outdoor-reared, with as much freedom as we could give them; petted, pampered, cuddled and chatted to on a daily basis. Hens (well, one in particular whom we called Atilla the Hen) wandered into our back kitchen to see what she could scrounge from Merryck's food bowl (not much - as a Retriever he was pretty much a furry vacuum cleaner), lambs, and then sheep, mowed our tearoom lawns and caravan site in the winter, (and did less than accurate pruning of any remaining shrubs) and, as mentioned, we'd even taken Cassie for a walk. (I once saw her strolling across the car park with one piglet in tow whilst I was serving cream teas in the tearoom. Knowing that our main gates were always open I tried to alert Keith whilst not alarming any of the guests. It's not often you see a pig as large as a sofa ambling towards your car).

Self-sufficiency with meat is not easy and means you have to try several sources. After we'd been at Spillers for a year or two Keith gained a shotgun licence. And then a shotgun. We thought that this might increase our meat sources, so that we could eat the meat that Keith managed to shoot from the skies or anywhere else. It was not a high tally. One or two pheasants, a rabbit that didn't run fast enough and a squirrel. After plucking our first pheasant, gutting it and digging out the shot, we realised it was a lot of effort for very little.

Subsequently, we just cut out the breasts for casseroling. Skinning a rabbit is like a magic trick. You basically turn it inside out like a glove. As for squirrel, well, it doesn't go far. We supplemented the virtually all-pork diet with Faverolles, a breed of chicken specifically bred to be shown - or eaten. Sounding like a dancing troupe, the Faverolles had feathery feet giving the impression they were wearing woolly socks. They were much larger and heavier than our egg-laying girls and much, much more flamboyant in their dress. They were the Liberace of hens. I don't remember them laying an egg. I think they thought that was beneath them.

We tried to live by the rule if we didn't grow it, we didn't manage it entirely; dairy was an issue. We did consider getting some goats for milk and cheese as previously mentioned, but as we were surrounded by dairy farmers that might have seemed crass. And besides, goats are like Houdini; fantastic escape artists, and I didn't think we had the energy to be fetching goats from neighbouring fields. We were virtually self-sufficient in our fruit, vegetables and meat. And it is a sad fact that if you are going to eat meat something has to die. As I've mentioned previously because we've taken the animal's life, we tried to honour that life by eating everything so we ate quite a lot of offal. Many people these days would turn their nose up at liver, kidneys and heart and yet they are all delicious, in fact the heart of any animal is the one that works constantly, making it incredibly 'meaty' and very tasty. I've probably lost all the vegetarians at this point. I probably lost the vegans on page one by mentioning the cream teas.

I have a great deal of sympathy with the vegetarian lifestyle (especially now that I don't have such good access to home-grown meat), but that is not what we were doing at the time. We were doing 'Compassionate Carnivorism'. We gave our animals the best possible life and the best possible death.

It was never nice. It was never a day we enjoyed. It's hard to take a creature you have seen born and load it onto a truck to drive it to its final destination. The final destination was a family-run abattoir about 10 minutes' drive from the farm. So, we comforted ourselves with the fact that they didn't have far to go and that their final journey was as stress-free as possible. The abattoir was run on the most compassionate lines possible; the animals taken in one by one, so they didn't have to watch each other die.

It was a proper smallholders' abattoir with a queue of smallholders' cars and vehicles lining up the driveway on certain days of the week. Keith recounts a story where he was queuing with a couple of pigs in the trailer when Terry Wogan started playing the Peter Gabriel song 'That'll Do Pig' - the theme song to the movie Babe. Finding tears running down his cheeks, he found another chap in tears at his window. Winding down the window, they looked at each other dabbing their eyes and the stranger asked with a sad smile, 'Listening to Terry Wogan too?'

And so, with great sadness we realised that Gollum and PF would also have to go there. They were by now getting on for three years old. They were past what could actually be termed lamb, and well on the way to becoming mutton. There are three stages: lamb (up to and just over one year), hogget, (one to two years) and mutton (anything older than that). To be honest I wish we ate more mutton and hogget in this country. Both are fantastic meats very well suited to slow cooking and sadly something we have lost contact with over the years. With PF I faced a real dilemma. I so wanted to keep her, just to cuddle her. Even though she had been sheared twice her fleece was still remarkably fluffy. She looked like a cloud on legs.

In fact, not only had she been sheared twice, but some of her fleece had been turned into wool. One of tearoom customers mentioned that she was in a spinning group and asked if she and her friends could bring their spinning wheels one day to make some wool on the tearoom lawns whilst having tea. (A quick diversion.... that lady and her husband came into the tearoom on a fairly regular basis, and we got to know them quite well. He had been a prisoner in a Japanese war camp and had suffered a great deal of deprivation during the Second World

War. As a consequence, he never went anywhere without a bit of bread in his pocket for fear of starvation.)

The spinning looked like a very enjoyable craft. Holding the fleece in one hand and rolling it back and forth as it spun on the wheel, becoming ever thinner and more uniform. Sheep fleece is naturally full of lanolin (makes them quite waterproof in the rain, it just falls off them, they are quite non-absorbent), so I imagine their fingers were quite soft. It was a pleasure to watch their skilful craft (although a bit like being in a fairy tale. I kept my fingers out of the way) and cheekily I asked if they could take a bit of PF's fleece - seeing as she'd not long been shorn. They did indeed take some, and cleverly turned it into a couple of balls of wool. I knitted myself a pair of fingerless gloves and a small scarf from the wool and wore them so that PF could meet herself. I wondered if she'd recognise the gloves as part of her. Would she be able to smell herself in the wool? She, naturally, took absolutely no notice.

But no barren sheep gets to live that long in the commercial world, and although we weren't completely in the commercial world, we were in the 'productive' world and our animals were our food. If we had let nature take its course, eventually she would have got really old, her teeth would have fallen out and she would have starved to death. Is that better? We threw this dilemma around for quite a while before the awful day when they were loaded and taken away.

It broke my heart. I dreamt about her that night. She was on the side of the road leading up to the abattoir staring at me and I woke up with a feeling like I'd swallowed a stone. Strange, but I wasn't that upset about Gollum. There was something about PF. I just loved her.

We drove to the abattoir the next day to pick up the lights (worst feeling in the world) and her all-important, wonderfully fluffy fleece. When we went to pick her up a few days later cut into pieces it was hard, but we had chosen this lifestyle and it left little room for sentimentalism. I made a mutton stew which I couldn't eat. The dog loved it. After she'd been in the freezer for a few months I tried again and bit by bit, bite by bite my lovely PF was gone.

But back to her fleece. For a few weeks we salted and dried the fleece on a rack in the garage. Then we took it to the nearest tanning factory, which was in Bridgwater, half an hour's drive away.

There were fleeces everywhere in this factory. And when I say everywhere I mean a warehouse-full, floor to ceiling piled high on top of each other. There were coats, slippers, boots, gloves, but most of all there were rugs and fleeces. There were literally thousands of them in every direction in all sorts of colours. Imagine my surprise then when we unrolled PF in front of the tanner. "Nice fleece," he said. We explained about PF and how we would like to remember her, especially her remarkable fleece. "Sheared twice you say?" the tanner looked at me with a surprised expression. "Yes," I said a little pride creeping into my voice as if I'd somehow had something to do with her fluffiness. "That is remarkable", the tanner continued. "Once a sheep has been sheared just once their fleece grows back much shorter and we tend to end up using them for gloves and slippers. To see a fleece like this after shearing twice is quite something." My heart nearly burst with pride! My PF! The world's fluffiest sheep! "I think she'll make a lovely rug", the tanner concluded.

And so she has. Every morning my feet swing out of bed onto a very large and still very fluffy rug. Pretty Fluffy Sheep has become Pretty Fluffy Rug. And when they come to put me in a nursing home PFR will be coming with me, rolled up under my arm.

THIS'LL BE THE END OF US!

"THIS'LL BE THE END OF US!" I yelled at Keith. I just didn't think I could do it anymore. Keith had always worked for himself, and experience told him, and so he told me, that the first five years would be the hardest. And boy were they ever. The first five years may have been the hardest, but the first six months nearly killed me. Six months after we moved to Spillers the strain of the massive mortgage we had taken on was beginning to show. We did everything we could think of to make the monthly payments.

Firstly, there was the existing business of the tearoom. We opened early at 8am serving breakfasts to passing workmen before the morning coffee crowd would start filtering in at 11. For them I had made a selection of four different types of cake: Carrot, Devonshire Apple, Lemon Drizzle and Tiffin. The first two courtesy of recipes from The AGA Queen, Mary Berry's AGA Cookbook, (Mary Berry was famous to me long before Bake Off). I'd never seen an AGA before arriving at the farm and the one in the kitchen was an enormous red, four-oven behemoth which was always on (particularly irritating in the long hot summers of 2005 and 2006, the latter being the hottest summer then on record since 1911). Without Mary Berry by my side, I don't know how I would have coped.

Whilst the coffee crowd were tucking into cake, I would be making a 'soup of the day', a hot daily special and a dessert and putting together salads for the lunch sandwiches. Once they were all served it was back to making more cakes (the apple cake in particular sold out fast) and of course making the ubiquitous scones. Keith and I once reckoned that we made and served 3,000 scones each season and without McDougals Scone Mix by my side I don't know how I would have coped. Because yes, dear reader, I cheated. A tearoom's reputation lives and dies on its scones and with everything else going on, the last thing I had time for was making sure the scones had risen. With Keith out the front telling everyone the scones (which were always highly praised) were based on an old family recipe, I would be pouring water onto scone mix and letting the Kenwood and the AGA do the rest.

We were really busy in the first two summers. So busy were we in fact that Keith didn't realise he'd lost his glasses for quite a while until he realised he couldn't focus. (We found them two years later turning over the compost heap. A bit bent, but still wearable). In the tearoom 4 o'clock was the height of the 'Cream Tea Rush'. This would be the peak time for people to come off the beach or break off their walk or whatever they were doing on their holiday and drive to Spillers for their cream tea. Often, the car park (which took about 20 cars) would be full and the tables inside and out (we had about six tables on the lawn) would be packed. Often was the time when I would see a large family group – or two – being led up the path towards the already packed tearoom by our resident Meeter and Greeter Merryck. Having just run out of scones my heart would temporarily sink before remembering that it was just ten minutes between pouring water on the scone mix and the newly arrived guests slathering clotted cream on their fresh-from-the-oven scones, and sigh with relief.

"How did you train him to do that?" the guests would often ask as Merryck would trot down the path towards the latest car to arrive, greet all the emerging occupants with a smile on his face and throw his body back towards the house and tearoom lawns by means of flinging both his front paws in that direction, whilst glancing over his shoulder at the guests with another smile before nodding towards the house and trotting up the path, all the while glancing back at the guests as if to say, "Welcome! Welcome, one and all. Great choice, Sir, Madam. You are just going to love it here. Ah, I see you have children. Fabulous. I love children." How did we train him to do that? We didn't. That was just him. He loved his job as Meeter and Greeter. The pay was lousy, but the Terms and Conditions were great.

As the gates were always open we would often get cars using the car park as a turning place for drivers who were lost (this was pre sat nav remember). Merryck would set off down the path and then a look of complete bafflement would replace his smile as he would watch the car depart as fast as it had arrived. Why would they not want to stop in this most perfect of establishments? We used to call these cars "The Turners" prompting one friend who was staying with us to ask how we knew their names.

The children Merryck loved the most were the toddlers. The younger members of the tribe who don't realise the necessity of holding onto one's food. For toddlers, food is as much about exploration of the world as it is fuel, and so a bit of cake or slice of teacake could often be waved

about and squished in a hand before the holder
might decide to put it in their mouth. Merryck was
always to be found lurking around these guests.
Sensing that the holder didn't really want to put the
food into their own mouth as much as he wanted to
put it in his, he would take it - very, very gently, but
quite definitely - and it would be gone. This would in
turn put an expression of complete bafflement on
the face of the child, and more often than not would
lead to tears and replacement cake being proffered.

But nobody really seemed to mind, as Merryck was
the gentlest and most lovable dog and the Spillers
inhabitant who got most mentions on Trip Advisor.
He was such an adept hustler at the tearoom tables
that we eventually had to put a poem on the
menus:

  When Merryck the dog begs you for some food,

  Please just ignore him; he won't think you rude.

  You see, we do feed him and don't want him fat.

  So, refuse all his pleadings. Just give him a pat!

I could watch from the kitchen window without
being seen and would see Merryck going from table
to table, plonking himself down beside the guests
but looking up and giving them 'the eyes' for a
morsel of cake or (his particular favourite) a scone.
Despite the poem, he was successful about 60% of
the time, and so I would shout to Keith, "Table 16

feeding the dog, Table 16". And then I'd watch as after a brief conversation with Keith, the occupants of Table 16 would shake their heads and deny all knowledge of feeding the dog currently licking his lips at their side.

I was quite happy spending my days in the kitchen though. (Apart from one incident due to the heat in those first two summers which meant we had to have the windows wide open to let some of the AGA heat out, leading to one tearoom customer bring her child to the window to watch me, saying, "Look at the lady in the kitchen," as if I was an exhibit in some sort of pre-emancipation museum.) I used to describe myself as the Scotty to Keith's Captain Kirk. Kirk may have been the one out front, the one everyone remembers, the one going boldly where nobody had gone before, but nobody would have got anywhere without Scotty doing all the work, quietly toiling away in the engine room. Keith is very likeable and has a very easy charm – imagine a slightly more legal Del Boy (human, not porcine) – and every day I would hear him regaling everyone with his tales of life on the farm; his stock phrases, "there's no money in pigs" and "to live this lifestyle you've got to have three things: passion, commitment and hard work", while I dusted flour off my hands and wished my feet didn't ache so much.

The summer season started in April, or March, or pretty much whenever Easter happened to fall. It would start with families, some of whom came to our cottage, some who just came into the tearoom on their way through to Cornwall, some who came in their caravans. After the families left there would be a slight lull before the May Bank Holidays. The first was never that busy. We used to call it the B&Q weekend. Falling quite soon after Easter that weekend would be quieter as (we assumed) most people spent that weekend decorating. But the late May Bank Holiday would really get the season going. Walkers, couples, grandparents with grandchildren, campers, honeymooners, we saw them all. The season would continue in June with our regulars, both regular tearoom customers and cottage guests who returned year after year, some of whom are now very good friends. Of particular note were Paul and Clare who looked after the farm for us one year whilst we went on holiday. They subsequently went on to have their own smallholding. It is an infectious lifestyle. Kim and her mum Jean came to the cottage every year without fail and were always first to come and feed the lambs. And finally, Glyn and Anne who came to have a cream tea and ended up as B&B guests, cottage guests and now lifelong friends. Glyn is a wonderful photographer and took some brilliant shots of our livestock. One of his photographs of Rodders was seen by an Amercian friend of his and she ordered a copy for her desk. Strange to think that our pig may still be gazing out at someone in a US office.

But I came to dread the end of July. I could picture

it. A line of traffic snaking past Stonehenge along the still single lane A303 all heading to the glorious Jurassic coastline. And who can blame them? We lived in an Area of Outstanding Natural Beauty which extended to real jewels on the coast like the stunningly beautiful Lyme Regis. We called them 'grockles', a West Country term for tourist, and they swarmed in and took over for the school holidays. Nobody local moves from the end of July until the beginning of September. We moved of course. In and out, in and out, constantly serving teas, coffees, cakes, scones, trying to make 12 months' money in six weeks. There were no days off, it was 42 days straight. Long hours, day after day, week after week. The goal was to get to the August Bank Holiday. If we could just make it to that weekend, things might tail off. If we could just make it. We did make it every year, but it was utterly exhausting. That first year the August Bank Holiday nearly killed us as we were used to it. We made about £500 on the Bank Holiday Monday and we thought we were Jeff Bezos. I remember walking to the lake at the end of the day where we liked to sit and have five minutes peace, and we were so exhausted it felt like I was climbing Everest.

But, as soon as August was out of the way and the children went back to school, out came their grandparents. September was still a beautiful month in the valley and it seemed to be the month of choice for the older generation. It wasn't really until October that things started to quiet down.

August was the only month that we argued. Exhaustion and stress take their toll and the only people we could take it out on was each other. It's really hard to have a decent argument whilst your house is full of strangers. We used to have these really heated discussions in hoarse stage whispers by the AGA, glaring at each other whilst putting together cream teas, then replacing our scowls with a fixed grin and floating into the tearoom as if we were having the time of our lives. Living the dream.

We made it all look very easy because we did have the passion and the commitment, and we were not afraid of hard work. Someone else who was not afraid of hard work and in fact, worked as hard as we did was Mariusz. After we'd been at Spillers for a month or two, we realised we were out of our depth. We needed a tearoom assistant, a washer up, a handyman, a gardener, a decorator and someone to play with the dog when we didn't have time. Mariusz was all these and more. His girlfriend, Renata, who had moved to Seaton from Poland a couple of months' previously, very cleverly sent out a general email asking if anyone had any work for her boyfriend. We answered, and pretty soon Mariusz arrived and was installed in the caravan that was proving and would continue to prove incredibly useful accommodation. He worked like a trooper and did everything we asked of him (except weeding). As well as being an incredibly hard worker, he was also enormous fun and had a great sense of humour. He had a willingness to learn and would test my knowledge of English by asking awkward questions. One day, whilst he was sweeping the floor at the end of the day he asked me, "What am I doing?" I said, "you're sweeping the floor." "Am I not brushing the floor?" "Well, yes, you are." "So, what is difference? Am I brushing or sweeping?" Etymological quizzes became part of our daily routine. Mariusz soon outgrew our little farm, and he moved to Seaton, married the beautiful Renata, and now he has two children and his own business. He really helped us in our early days and probably saved us from a complete breakdown on a number of occasions.

We had a whole host of regulars that would visit in those early years. Kathy, a lady who had contracted polio in her thirties and no longer had use of her legs but would drive in her specially adapted car and park at the end of the path to have lunch in her car. Kathy was full of stories. Friends with famous cricketing umpire Dickie Bird, she had once been chased round the deck of the Queen Mary by Count Basie. Colin and his wife Stephanie who once told me she couldn't have anything to eat on account of the cocaine the dentist had just given her. Amazing what you can get on the National Health these days. There was the chap who was a gamekeeper and asked us if we'd like him to bring in some venison next time he visited. We greedily snapped up his offer and the next week he arrived at our back door with a skinned version of Bambi.

No head, no hooves, no skin, but Bambi none the less.

But our most regular of regulars were Neville and Winnie who came at least once a week, if not twice. Watching them arrive the first time I could see them having a frantic conversation about what Winnie (a committed smoker) was to do with her fag end before they reached the door until I wandered out to meet them holding a large scallop shell the previous owner had used as her own ashtray. They weren't a couple, both had been widowed, but they enjoyed day trips together and we were always the first port of call. Winnie for a cheese and onion toastie and Neville for a toasted teacake.

However, even if Winnie and Neville did come twice a week, the tearoom wasn't making enough to meet our massive mortgage. So, we started to open on Friday and Saturday nights.

FRIDAY NIGHT DINNER

I watched Sila, one of our recently acquired black and white kittens effortlessly standing on her back paws, whilst playing with a dancing cranefly with those at her front, by the open back door as the light began to fade on what had been a beautiful late September Friday. I envied her energy. For Friday and Saturday nights for me had become an exhausting round of pretending I was some sort of trained chef.

As five o'clock came round on Friday and Saturday evenings we would clear the remains of the quaint tearoom cups and saucers (mainly sourced from charity shops – you know the ones, the ones that your granny used to drink from, pretty porcelain sets that would now be described as kitsch), throw some tablecloths on the tables and turn it into what might be overly generously described as a 'bistro'.

As this was happening, I would often be having a not-particularly-well-disguised panic attack in the kitchen. I would have prepared - and for the next few hours would be continuing to prepare - dinner for around 20 strangers. Three choices of starter, main course and dessert. I quite liked cooking, but this was on another level, and it probably says more about the paucity and lack of places to eat in the vicinity at the time than my culinary expertise. I can only be grateful that Trip Advisor had not yet reached our shores (and much more about that hellish creation later), or I very much doubt that we would have been doing it for more than two weeks.

As it was, we managed to pull off this remarkable bistro con trick for a few months leading up to Christmas. It was this feat of endurance on my part which led to me yelling at Keith that this would end us. It was the most exhausting and emotionally draining experience and now I have such incredible respect for those in the catering industry. It is a hard job with anti-social hours, not easy on the feet and often impossible to meet the expectations of those on the other side of the kitchen doors.

However, buoyed by the fact that people kept returning to eat at Spillers, we thought we'd give Christmas lunch a go. Christmas lunch. The most important meal of the year. What could possibly go wrong?

OF MICE AND MEN

Christmas 2005 was a magical, snowy affair. Apparently, it had not snowed in the area for 15 years, so we more than fortunate to see it in our first year. Having lived in the Highlands of Scotland for several years in his twenties, for Keith the sight of pristine fields devoid of footprints in every direction was nothing special, but for me - a city girl through and through - it was the most amazing sight. I used to love walking to the lake and watching Merryck play in the snow, throwing him snowballs which he would expertly catch and dissemble before trying to eat them. A couple of years later it snowed again and was so cold for so long that the lake froze, the frost becoming so hard and thick that after a month we were able to walk across it. But the locals were right, it was rare, and in the rest of our time there we never lucky enough to see snow again.

To help us out with our rash decision to cook the year's most important meal for 30 paying strangers we had turned to our friends Mike and Su. Mike was an old school friend of Keith's. They had lost touch but had found each other again just before we left London due to the precursor of Facebook, a website called Friends Reunited, which had indeed reunited them. Mike was a competent amateur cook, and his lovely and bubbly wife Su would be great at front of house with Keith.

As further help we had bought an extra gas oven and installed it next to the red behemoth that was the AGA.

Mike and Su arrived on Christmas Eve. Eyeing the new gas oven Mike turned to me and said: "You've cooked using both of these already, right?" "Err, no, not yet" I nervously replied. "Why?" "Well, they're both using the same gas pipe," continued Mike as if this explained everything. "And?" I nervously replied. "Well, when they're both being used there may not be enough gas for both of them, so everything will cook pretty slowly." So much for our best-laid plans. "It'll probably be alright", he said. Now it was Mike's turn to sound nervous.

Most of that Christmas Eve was spent prepping. We had 30 guests, so that meant three pieces of potato each, 90 pieces in all. We decided there would be plenty of leftovers so didn't make extra for us. (We regretted that the next day as we all shared a single roast potato!) But let me tell you, it takes some time to peel and cut enough potatoes to make 90 pieces, let alone carrots, parsnips, alongside preparing a mound of stuffing balls and getting 90 pigs into their blankets, but once we were finished, we went for a walk in the countryside. As we walked past the lake Su was very taken by the swans that were sussing out the lake as a prospective home for their batch of cygnets. As we had lived in the countryside all of seven months and now being considerably wiser in the way of the countryside now than these two town interlopers, Keith regaled Su with the benefits of swan's milk. It's very rare but very nutritious. He also pointed out the Siberian Stillduck in the middle of the lake. We had found a decoy duck abandoned in one of Farmer Edwards' fields on a walk one day. It had probably become stranded after a bit of field flooding and we decided to rehome it by tying it to a very heavy weight and throwing it in our lake to see if it would attract any local wildlife. It did. Many was the bewildered Mallard that flew in and tried to chat it up. It also proved a source of amusement (for us) telling Su and other townies to look out for any signs of movement. The Stillduck is a totally unflappable creature and will rarely move – if at all, although underneath the water its feet are paddling like mad just to keep it in the same spot. When we returned from our walk, Su was amazed to see the duck in exactly the same spot and probably spent all

Christmas watching out for signs of movement.

Halfway round the walk I remembered the batch of mince pies I had put in the oven prior to setting out. It is the lot of many an AGA owner I imagine, but because you can neither see, hear or smell the food in the AGA, it is possible to forget an entire batch of mince pies until you are at least 20 minutes' walk from your house. By the time we returned, the mince pies had carbonised into small intensely black balls that not even the pigs would enjoy. And I started to make another batch of pastry.

But eventually it was the night before Christmas and all through the house, nobody was stirring, not even a mouse. Well, perhaps a mouse, one mouse in particular. And me. I couldn't sleep. What's the one meal in the whole year that you can't mess up? Christmas lunch. What's the one meal that I was preparing - not for loving and forgiving friends and family - but for fee-paying customers? Christmas lunch. It was a terrifying prospect.

But it was alright. Sort of. The first guests arrived at 11.45am for a lunch that we said would be served at 1pm. I think Mike and I were probably still peeling the sprouts at that point, watching the spuds as they refused to brown no matter what oven they were in whilst Keith and Su were laying up tables. Nerves gave way to adrenaline as the guests arrived, the tearoom filled up and the sound of happy chatter and the songs from a 'Now That's What I Call Christmas 385' CD filled the place. As we started plating up and delivering the food, things seemed to go well. I had spent the entire month preparing for this particular feast making everything from scratch. I'd made two Christmas puddings, lots of mince pies (even more because of the ones I'd burnt), my own cranberry and bread sauces, plus a brandy sauce to accompany the puddings. I'd enjoyed the process and followed Delia Smith's instructions to the letter, so what could possibly go wrong?

I actually began to relax as the last pudding went out to the waiting (and now very boisterous sounding) customers and began to fill the dishwasher, singing along with Nat King Cole about his roasting chestnuts. I pressed the start button on the dishwasher and.... BANG! Everything stopped. The dishwasher, the singing, the music, the lights, my heart. All stopped. "Quick", I yelled to Su and Mike, "get out there! Make sure they don't notice!" as Keith fiddled furiously with the fuse board. I joined them out front, full of smiles and Christmas cheer. Fuelled by wine, Baileys, Cognac and goodness knows what else they had brought (it was a strictly BYOB affair) the guests were now talking and laughing so loudly I don't think they had even noticed we were playing music, let alone the fact that it had stopped. After a few minutes it all cranked up again and nobody seemed to be any the wiser. Keith had discovered the fault. A mouse had been living in our dishwasher during our downtime when it wasn't used that much and had chewed through some wiring. As soon as we put the dishwasher on it had short-circuted. So much for the mouse's best-laid plans.

By about 5 o'clock we had just about finished the washing up and the last happy revellers were tipsily making their way to their cars, and it was time for our Christmas lunch. Exhausted though we were, we still found the energy for a game of charades before prepping to do something similar the next day for other paying guests who'd opted for a Boxing Day lunch. To this day it is still one of my favourite Christmases.

CAMPING EXPEDITION

Christmas comes but once a year, so one Christmas might have paid the December mortgage, but by the next summer we were still struggling. Relief seemed to appear in the shape of a TV company who were filming a reality TV show in Colyton, a small town nearby, and needed accommodation for the crew for six weeks. We leapt at the chance and gave them every room in the house – including our own.

So where were we to sleep? We tried a friend's caravan at first. Our friend Andy had visited in our first summer. I think he was the first to pitch on our CL site, and rather than drag his definitely-seen-better-days-van back home, he asked if he could store it in the corner of our field. He never came back for it and let us have it. Mariusz had lived in it for a while and now it became a refuge for us for a week or two. But we had to give it up because Mike came back. Not having had enough exhaustion over Christmas he came back to help us out in our first full summer season, meaning that we had to give up the van. We were happy to do so, we were in need of help, but now where we going to sleep? In a borrowed tent of course! Where better to lay your head after an exhausting day on your feet? The two-man tent was erected in the field a little distance from the house and at the end of the day we would trudge out to it by the light of a lantern and a torch, get into our sleeping bags and settle down to sleep. Or rather not to sleep. Our dog Merryck, who was quite young at the time, would spend most of the night nudging us awake and setting off back towards the house. We'd drag him back with him looking over his shoulder at the house as if to say: "We've got this really big house over there. Look, it's really comfortable and huge. Much bigger than this canvas triangle. I really don't understand why we're here and not there." Meanwhile, our two kittens (procured from Martha - Edward's ancient farm cat's - latest litter), were having the time of their lives chasing each other round and round the gap between the inner and outer linings of the tent. Any sleep we did get was regularly disturbed by having your head bashed by one, then the other, as they sped past our not-quite-sleeping forms. Thankfully it was once again a glorious summer; long, hot, sunny days without a spec of rain. But six weeks of sleeping in a tent made me so grateful for my bed. No matter how much we had to work, I never wanted to try the big camp out again.

BIRDS OF A FEATHER

The Summer of the Tent was before we had hens.
We already had ducks. They had been procured
by Keith whilst I had returned to London for a
weekend to visit my sister. I came back on the
Sunday night to the news that we had a dozen
ducks and a drake now resident in a small shed by
the field nearest the house. Peering through the
window at them I was amazed how big they
seemed. Somehow, I had imagined ducks were
the same size as those yellow plastic ones you see
bobbing around your bath. These looked enormous
and I asked Keith if he was sure they weren't

geese? But I came to love them and their eggs. Duck eggs are larger than hen's and have wonderful golden creamy yolks, not very much white. Great for cakes. Rubbish for meringues.

The sound of the ducks quacking as they formed a line and followed each other up to the lake when we let them out of the shed, and the sight of them waddling back at dusk each night became part of the aural backdrop of Spillers. They always reminded me of a bunch of gossiping women busying their way to or from a factory as if their quacking was them exchanging news, "Did you hear what she said?" "Oooh, then what happened?". And there was the occasional burst of quacking from the lake which sounded just like a burst of laughter, as if one of them had just told the others a particularly hilarious joke.

There is something very calming about watching animals go about their business. Sitting at the lake watching the ducks preen and wash themselves every morning could be very calming. They are very fastidious, cleaning every feather, and the incredible flexibility of their necks as they reach backwards towards their tailfeathers is something at which to marvel. Something else at which to marvel about ducks is their love of slugs and snails. If you have any hostas in your garden, get a duck! They are fantastic at rootling around soft leaves and finding slugs, snails and other creepies and because their beaks are soft and round, they don't damage the plants. We had planted a hosta at the lake. It grew to an enormous size and the leaves were always perfect due to the fastidiousness of the anatidae gardeners.

We had two drakes, one Aylesbury, one Mallard. The Mallard was a lovely looking bird and we called our him Sir Francis; the original Drake having had some sort of local connection. Our neighbour Farmer Edwards' farm was called Drakes Farm and it was situated opposite the village pub – The Golden Hind. There was also an effigy in Musbury village church to members of the Drake family in full Elizabethan doublet and hose.

We had a combination of Mallards, Aylesburys and Indian Runners. Mallards are your general standard duck. For Aylesburys think Donald. For Indian Runner think Jemima Puddleduck (although none of them wore bonnets or carried wicker baskets). Runners tend to hang together very tightly for security and turn as one, this way and that, which makes them ideal for training sheepdogs apparently, and (as you will remember) a complete nightmare when you're trying to get them out of the lake and back on to dry land.

At first the ducks lived in the brick garage by the lake field, but once we had decided to get hens and put them in the garage, we needed somewhere to else for the ducks. As we scanned the field for ideas our eyes fell upon the abandoned caravan in which we'd camped out briefly and decided it would be a perfect duck house. We stripped it out and filled the bottom with straw. That was the easy part. Getting the ducks to move in was nigh on impossible. They don't seem to like change, and they definitely didn't like the caravan. But we funnelled them into it and left them there for 24 hours enabling them to get used to it. One of my funniest memories of the ducks is seeing a head and neck silhouetted in the back window of the van looking confused like an accidental tourist.

The combination of light, fleet of webbed foot ducks and heavier breeds led to some unusual pairings. Runner ducks are small and light, Mallards and Aylesburys not so much, and this caused problems with mating. Ducks mating can look pretty brutal. The male duck grabs the female by the feathers on the back of her neck and climbs aboard. This is fine (well, I wouldn't like it much) when they're in the water where they tend to do most of their 'courting', as the water holds the weight of both bodies, although it does tend to look like the male is drowning the female, but it causes problems on land as the male Aylesbury/Mallard is much heavier than his Indian Runner girlfriend. Plus, males seem to have an insistence that their seed is the one to succeed, so if one of the males had had a go, the others have to do the same. Sadly, this meant that for one poor Indian Runner girl, the weight of her second or third encounter with Sir Francis (the mallard) or the Donald (the Aylesbury) was so much that he broke her leg. Unable to get up from this ordeal, we took her 'under our wing' (as it were) and made her a splint by strapping a bit of wood to her leg. Ever resilient, she learned to walk with the splint and when we removed it, she always walked with a limp. Ever after to be known as Limpy, she outlived her compatriots and was still at Spillers Farm when we left about eight years later. I can still see her making her own distinct way to the lake. She would trail just after the rest of the flock with her bad leg stuck out behind her and the opposite wing sticking out as a counterbalance in a fast, limping trot.

And what became of her boyfriend? Well, such behaviour was not to be tolerated. We chopped his head off.

THE EXECUTIONER'S FINGER, OR THE COCKEREL'S REVENGE.

We became quite adept at chopping their heads off. (Dispatching them is the more correct term), but that first time was quite terrifying. It was probably pretty scary for the bird too. I may have had quite a supervisory role for many smallholding tasks, but I was actively involved in the dispatch. We developed a process where once we'd caught the bird (no mean feat in itself, young birds are fast runners), I held onto the body, laid it down on a big block of wood and Keith would grab hold of the head and bring an axe swiftly down on the neck. It was quick. It was humane. And (we told ourselves) they didn't know what was coming. The birds themselves almost became philosophical about it, quietening down and seeming to accept their fate. And it's true what they say about headless chickens running around. Well, almost. They don't run very far, or for very long and it's more of a stumble about than an organised jog, but the headless body does flail about for a bit. It's quite disconcerting. And most alarming of all - and something peculiar to the ducks – the detached head would turn around on the ground to look directly at its dispatcher and the beak would move as if it was trying to talk. It was like a finger pointing directly at you – J'accuse! J'accuse!

Talking of fingers, Keith nearly chopped his off one day. I was kneeling on the ground holding the chicken's body near the block. Keith raised the axe and just before he brought it down to deliver the final blow, it moved. And Keith chopped off a bit of his finger instead of the head. Dropping the bird (who started to run about sideways with half its head hanging off), Keith handed me the axe. I stared at the piece of flesh on the axe which used to be attached to Keith and tried not to panic. "Look, we're going to have to finish it off," I said, and we both made a grab for the bird. By now there was plenty of blood around (from the bird or from Keith it was hard to tell), and unfortunately it was a white bird, so it was getting messy. We grabbed the bird and Keith raised the axe again, a little less steadily. But this time we ensured it was over and then we ran inside and took the bit of his finger off of the blade. Wrapping it in cling film and his hand in a bit of kitchen roll, he drove off to the local hospital, whilst I cleaned up the blood and feathers and tried not to feel sick.

A few minutes later I saw him driving past the door again with his left hand up in the air still covered in swathes of kitchen roll. Managing to get him on the phone he explained that the local hospital had told him to get himself to Exeter Hospital about 20 miles away. Apparently, because of the proliferation of farming accidents in the area, Exeter Hospital is one of the best hospitals in the country for hand surgery. I was still shaking from the whole experience, but Keith (driving one handed) was taking it in his stride. I can only imagine he was in shock like those stories you hear of where farmers' arms are ripped off and they calmly walk across the field with the detached limb under their arm.

By the time he was seen at the hospital, a consultant took the bit of skin we had tremblingly wrapped in cling film and threw it in the bin. "If you'd been here within half an hour" he said, "we could have used that. But now, it's dead." Tell that to the chicken I thought. He was offered a skin graft from his thigh, but instead opted for the skin just to grow back. It has done and he carries a nasty scar to this day. Still a better outcome than for the chicken.

We only dispatched the males. It is a truism that in the animal kingdom it is not a good thing to be born male. Very few are needed. At the height of our chicken-keeping we had 50 hens and two cockerels, and one of them only stayed by default. Males are not really needed and too many males (especially cockerels) can lead to fighting. It was only once I started keeping poultry that I'd taken any notice of chicken's feet. Cockerels have massive feet and about halfway up their legs they have a spur, an extra toe which looks like it's deliberately there for fighting. We did have two cockerels at one time in one pen, but not for long. Within minutes, they were both obviously competing for territory and started flying at each other with their legs up, trying to cut each other with their spurs. Typical blokes really.

We had rescued some ex-battery hens and after they had recovered, we found we would need a cockerel to keep them in order. Our first and most handsome cockerel was given to us. Most cockerels are given away. They're noisy, full of themselves to the point of cockiness (I wouldn't be surprised if that's where the term comes from), a bit useless without a hen house to run, and worst of all, they don't lay eggs.

They eat without giving anything back.

Apparently, birds are descended from dinosaurs, and this is very clear when you've seen an ex-battery hen. Battery farmers tend to keep their sheds very warm, thus the birds don't need to grow feathers and all their energy goes into egg laying. Our first batch of 20 or so hens were a very sorry sight and looked almost exactly like smaller versions of the Velociraptors in Jurassic Park. Almost completely featherless, most of them looked oven-ready, but with pale faces and even paler combs and wattles. They had a scared look about them. We picked them up from the local agent for the Battery Hen Welfare Trust, an organisation which takes battery hens that the industry no longer needs. The industry no longer needs them because after 12 months a hen will naturally start to lay fewer eggs and as profit is the name of the game in battery egg production, the hens are either slaughtered (I imagine for dog food – the chicken in dog food isn't going to be first class chicken breast) or given to charities such as the BHWT.

However, they are not completely beyond egg-laying, in fact one of them laid an egg in the back of the car on the way home! We took them home and settled them in a small garage that we had converted to a very large and fairly luxurious hen house. They didn't come out of the garage for three days. Not having ever really seen the light of day, they had no real idea how to behave, but it was a joyful sight after a few days to see one or two of the bravest hens give into their curiosity and poke their heads out of the door. Within a week they were all out, scratching the earth and feasting on the grass and any insects they could find. All the while they were free roaming to their hearts' content and laying eggs in straw covered nesting boxes. They had found Hen Heaven.

But you can get problems with a load of ladies living on their own. Sooner or later, you will get a dominant hen who wants to rule the roost. You can really see the hierarchy in a hen house, and it is sorted out with pecking. It truly is a 'pecking order'. The top hen will peck the next one down, so on and so on until there is one poor hen at the bottom of the ladder who is picked on by all and sundry. The dominant hen can be disruptive, doing things like blocking the doorway of the hen house and causing any number of issues. So, we decided we needed a manager, and our friends Chris and Sue were giving away a cockerel. Chris and Sue also had a farm nearby and we had found each other through the local village gossip grapevine that preceded Facebook. Chris and Sue were our closest friends during those years and the only people with whom we had any conversation with that wasn't totally superficial small talk but was (thanks to Sue) largely peppered with innuendo.

They arrived with a youngish cockerel in a cat carrier, and we put him in a shed near the garage which had a round hole in one of the walls. Looking through that hole we could just see the cockerel's head sideways on, looking for all the world like the image on the Cornflakes packet. He was instantly named Kellogg.

Poor Kellogg had a real baptism of fire. He had 25 recovering Velociraptors to control, and at first the youngster had a hard time, but nature took control, and he soon was Lord and Master of the house. It is a fascinating thing to see nature's natural hierarchy. In every case, from cats to pigs but especially with the chickens, the men are in charge. A cockerel keeps a well-run hen house and once he had gained dominance there was no more fighting. If a dispute did break out between hens, Kellogg would be swiftly on the scene dispensing justice with a head peck to each hen in turn, who would immediately stop squabbling and follow him wherever he went. It was fascinating to watch him make sure that everyone had something to eat. If we threw in some greens or other sort of treat, he would call to the girls using a particular cluck which indicated food, not stopping until they had all had the chance to get some of the goodies, before taking any for himself if there was any left. If there was danger from above, a buzzard or even a plane, Kellogg would use a different sort of call and urge his ladies to take shelter in the house until the danger had passed, running behind them with his wings outstretched pushing them into safety. Buoyed by Kellogg's success at ruling the roost we got a further 25 hens and he took that all in his stride, strolling around the field with his massive hareem and generally loving his life as literally cock of the walk.

Having a cockerel changed the pecking order. He was definitely Number One, but he also had his favourites. He would team up with a hen now and again who he really favoured and got special treatment. The most special treatment was where they would sleep. We put an old wooden ladder which reached from wall to wall in the hen house garage where most of the hens would perch at night. Kellogg's perch was right in the middle of the ladder and the most coveted sleeping places were right next to him. If we went into the hen house at night you could see at least 18 of the hens looking for all the world like a mass of giant budgies, trying to cram right up next to Kellogg. How they managed not to fall off is beyond me.

This reminds me of a useful tip if you're ever trying to move your hens from one shed to another. From time to time, we would have to isolate a bird who was unwell or move some birds for some reason. At first, we tried to do this during the day and spent many fruitless hours running after the birds who were much more fleet of foot than us and without a large version of a fishing net, it's an almost impossible task. After a few years we cottoned on to moving them at night. As they settle for the night (hens naturally roost at dusk, they take themselves off to bed), they become calm, almost doped and can be picked up and carried away offering no resistance.

Word gets around in small communities, and people in the nearby village knew that we had brought animals back to Spillers. This led to people occasionally bringing random animals to us for 'safekeeping'. The lake had already been stocked with the contents of someone's goldfish tank before we moved in, and now we were ready for our own donation of randoms. One day a woman turned up with a Bantam hen and her offspring. The hen had 10 chicks in tow, so we immediately named her Angelina and the Jolie-Pitts. We settled them in the small shed where we had settled all the creatures that had arrived; the ducks, then Kellogg and now the Bantams. Bantams are attractive little birds, much smaller than the usual domestic hen, but fierce fighters (hence Bantam-weight boxers). As Angelina and her crew settled in, we were delighted to see that some of the chicks were female and in time we were able to offer our B&B guests another type of egg for their breakfast; hen's, duck's or Bantam hen's, something I don't think I've ever seen on a B&B breakfast menu. We were less than delighted to see that the majority of the chicks were males. The last thing we needed was a bunch of cockerels around the place.

It is incredibly hard to sex a chick or duckling when it has just emerged. I'm sure more experienced experts could do it easily, but it was way above our pay grade. It was always disappointing whenever we or a broody hen hatched chicks or we hatched ducklings and after a few weeks we could see their plumage and tails beginning to look distinctly male. We used to hope against hope that our eyes were deceiving us and what was definitely beginning to look like male plumage was just an optical illusion, because if they were turning into blokes there was only one end – they'd end up in the oven. We would watch these teenage poultry running round the field and say to ourselves, "nah, they're females, it's going to be OK" trying to ignore the bright colours and curling tail feathers*. A couple of days later we'd have to admit it. It's a bunch of casseroles running around the field.

But we also noticed that the Bantams were great wanderers. They wandered much further than the other poultry. You'd find them in the vegetable garden, up by the lake, on the front lawn.... they were much more adventurous than the other birds who were kept in line by Kellogg, but unfortunately this meant that fewer and fewer of them came home each night, most likely ending up as a fox's dinner. Ten chicks plus mum, got whittled down eventually to just one, a cockerel with a beautiful golden mane of plumage around his neck. He had survived, he didn't wander, he clearly thought of this as home. So, we had to keep him.

Obviously, this was Cornflake.

Maybe it was a size thing; as a Bantam, Cornflake was so much smaller than Kellogg the Welsummer, and so they never fought. Cornflake had a habit of jumping onto a fencepost and singing his very high-pitched crow. In fact, that became my morning alarm call. I would wake in the dark just before dawn and listen. Fairly soon I would hear Kellogg's "Cock-a-da-daaaah", immediately followed by the same sound from Cornflake about an octave higher "Cock-a-de-daaah". It gave me a great sense of satisfaction to know that my boys were safe and well and had kept their ladies safe and well all night.

Cockerels' crowing makes a great deal of sense in the countryside. Our nearest neighbours were about half a mile away across two fields - Farmer Edward and his son Robert and family, the Gays. Not the only Gays in the village, as his other son Richard was the neighbour on our other side, another half a mile away across another two fields. One of the cockerels would start the call, either Kellogg or a cockerel at the Gays and they would crow back and forth to each other for a while. You could just about hear the Gay's cockerel crowing and they could probably just about hear Kellogg. The boys were warning each other, "This is my territory! Stay out of it!"

Cockerel crowing didn't mean that every animal stayed away from the hens however. It certainly didn't apply to rats. Grain and hen food are a particularly sought-after source of food for rats and the fact that we had an infestation became obvious one day at feeding time. Along the back wall of the hen house was a long piece of corrugated iron. Our method of settling the hens at night was to go in and throw food all over the floor, they would scratch for it and once eaten they would settle down to sleep. I was merrily throwing food all over the place, some of which was hitting the corrugated iron - and that seemed to be the cue. At that sound, dozens of rats poured over the top of the corrugated iron and started scratching around on the floor with the hens. It's a mark of how far I had turned from city slicker into country girl that I didn't immediately scream, "RATS!, AAAAARRRGGH!, RATS! RATS! HELP!" and start looking for a chair to stand on. Instead, I calmly wondered to myself why it seems that it's only humans (maybe women in particular) that are scared of rats, as the hens didn't seem the slightest bit bothered by them. James Herbert and George Orwell have got a lot to answer for. I wasn't really scared. I just thought they looked like big mice. Really big mice.

So, I headed back to the house and said to Keith, "We've got a bit of a rat issue." To be honest it wasn't the first rat I'd seen. They didn't make themselves that obvious, but they were around. Quite often you'd hear a scuttling in the edges of the field, or something small and brown would quickly run past you at dusk as you were in the veg garden, but as long as they kept themselves to themselves we had a bit of a live and let live attitude to them.

And of course, we had our feline Pest Control Officers. The Ster (more of whom later) who was our male cat was particularly adept at rat catching and now and again I would come down to breakfast to find him at the back door, sitting proudly by a decapitated rat with a look of sheer delight on his face. He was like a Wild West Sheriff, adjusting the holster round his hips, pushing his hat up higher up his forehead, saying, "He won't be troublin' you again Mam".

But if there was a large family of them living in the hen house that couldn't be tolerated. I know it's not nice, but it's a lot nicer than us being closed down, so we got the poison out. (Now I've probably just lost the PETA crowd). One by one we found the dead rats and disposed of them. I remember finding one particularly large beast which must have been at least a foot long from head to tail. Grabbing him by the tail I carried him away from the hen house, feeling the weight of him swinging at my side as we walked across the field. How much I had changed. Once a city girl who wore heels, mascara and bought all her clothes from Karen

Millen, now I thought nothing of swinging a dead rat by the tail. Spillers was changing me.

In his dotage Kellogg seemed to team up with one of the oldest hens in the flock. They were always together, and quite often she would literally be standing underneath him and he'd have his wings wrapped around her. We started to call them Mr & Mrs. Unlike swans, poultry don't tend to mate for life, but it can happen apparently, and it certainly seemed to be the case with The Kelloggs. But it couldn't be denied that after many years of fantastic service, Kellogg (by now an old man) started to ail. His crow became less forceful and over a few weeks it was obvious he was dying. On his last day we found him draped over his girl in the morning and we knew he wouldn't last for much longer. And thus, one of the cruellest acts that happened during our time at Spillers started. Dissatisfied with his lack of authority and lacklustre attitude to their care, the hens turned on him. They started to peck him to death. Without the energy to fight back this would have been poor Kellogg's fate, but we intervened and took him away and let him die quietly in the shed where he had bedded down many years previously on his arrival. It was a sad day. We had become very fond of our lovely cockerel. We buried him on the island in the middle of the lake. Mrs Kellogg pined for him for two days then she died too. We wonder if she died of a broken heart. We buried her with her beau and he probably still has his wings wrapped around her.

It was obvious that a pipsqueak like Cornflake (himself well into middle age) couldn't control the girls, and so cockerel number three arrived at Spillers. This time we fancied a Leghorn (like Foghorn Leghorn of Looney Tunes cartoon fame), and a young, large perfectly white cockerel was sourced. Keeping the breakfast name theme this one was christened Krispie. However, he was a very different kettle of fish. He was a nasty piece of work, grabbing food before the girls and generally pushing he weight around. He was the one that started fighting as soon as he arrived. I didn't like him, and his attitude made me realise what a gent Kellogg had been. He was sorely missed.

However, Krispie wasn't the only bird with a bad attitude that we had at Spillers. Having cracked it in the hen and duck stakes, one year we decided to get some geese. We procured a small flock of four goslings, which turned into three dames (females) and a gander. We were delighted when they matured, and the girls started laying eggs and again could offer our B&B guests something unusual on the menu. However, it wasn't just the girls who matured. There was also that gander. And his swagger knocked anything the cockerels had into touch. He thought incredibly highly of himself. One day, I was coming back from the lake and passing through all the poultry, quietly free ranging and going about their business. The gander obviously took a disliking to me, or I walked a bit too closely to him, or he was just showing off, but he spread his wings widely and advanced. With his wings outstretched he seemed much larger and he probably stood around three feet tall with his neck stretched, so he was quite an imposing figure for someone who is not much over five feet tall. Unsure of what to do, I sort of stood there and watched him. He continued advancing and by now he was also making some sort of noise – if you understood geese speak he was probably using foul language (pardon the pun) - and he really wasn't backing down. Still standing in front of him, I kept thinking to myself, "But what harm can he do? He's not even got any teeth." However, the closer he got, the more nervous I became. He might not have had any teeth but he had a look in his eye which said, "I'm coming for you, even if I have to suck you to death, I'm coming for you." It worked. I started to run. He started to run. I ran faster. He ran faster. I just made it to the gate and slammed it behind me as he charged into it. I looked over the gate at him and he hissed back at me, with a look in his eye that told me I was not welcome to trespass on his property again. Quite breathless and more than a little intimidated I kept well-clear of him from then on.

We got our own back of course come Christmas when he was pride of place on our table for lunch.

* If memory serves there is a feather on the tail of the male duck which curls upwards and is distinctly male, and of course the plumage of the cockerel's

tail is quite something to see. Kellogg's tail feathers were particularly grand and so were those of his progeny.

CHRISTMAS

Christmas is coming, the turkey's looking tasty.

The turkey eyes the axe, says, "Now c'mon don't be hasty."

"It's your destiny," you say to the bird. "And you're so good for a feast.

But it's not just you who gets the chop, we'll also do the geese!"

I wrote that little ditty and it just about sums up life

at Spillers come December. It seems strange to me now that our annual celebration of the birth of Christ is mainly a tree and animal massacre, but that's Christmas!

Our dozen turkeys arrived as poults (basically baby turkeys – think of a turkey the size of a chicken), in August. They lived in what was called the Pole Barn, a large open-sided barn made of corrugated iron. They roosted and nested on bales of straw and basically just stood about staring at us. I don't have any expertise on the subject, but turkeys do appear to me to be a very stupid bird. They have a very small head compared to the size of their bodies. No not small; tiny. They have a tiny head and somewhere in that tiny head is a tiny brain. They are no great thinkers, but their talent for making things stinky is unsurpassed. Ours tended to do a lot of standing about and pooing, causing our grandson (then aged four) to call them the Pooey Turkeys. Their capacity to grow seemed also unsurpassed as they went from being the same size as the hens, then very quickly the same size as the geese, and within a few weeks they were seemingly not much smaller than the swans which nested on the lake each year.

Around mid-December it was time for them to fulfil their destiny and we backed the trailer into the Pole Barn and herded them in. We set off for Lorna's farm. Lorna's daughter was married to our neighbour Farmer Edward's son and probably related to him in some other way as well. That was another thing I was learning about the farming community into which I'd moved. They are all related. They're either cousins, or cousins of cousins, or married to a cousin, or in laws or something or other twice removed, but basically, they are all family. From Dorset to Somerset to Devon you'd only have to mention a name and they'd all know exactly who you were talking about and then mention that their Aunt/Sister/Brother/Nephew/Mother/Father/Cousin (especially cousin) was their cousin.

Lorna basically had the turkey market for the immediate 10-mile radius sewn up. She was like the Turkey Queen. If you liked to push a pun perhaps you could say she wore the Turkey Crown, but truth was if you bought a turkey from any butcher in the local area it came from Lorna's.

Turkey plucking at Lorna's was quite the set up. Beside what you might call a warehouse-sized pole barn that made ours look like a rabbit hutch, was a small room with wooden benches all around the edges. Seated on these benches was a group of farming types (no doubt all cousins of Lorna's), kitted out in the ubiquitous farmer's garment, the boiler suit. (Mine was blue and - until that day - pretty clean. I had the look of the novice turkey plucker about me). Every person in the room had a just-dead turkey on their lap with several more on the table in the centre of the room. Bloody feathers covered the floor, and I don't mean bloody feathers in a way that I found them irritating, I mean there was blood all over them. In fact, there were bloody feathers everywhere. All over the floor, all over the people and floating around in the air. The noise was cacophonous. For a start there was the gobbling of hundreds of turkeys in the warehouse. Then there was the noise from what I called 'the killing machine' next door in the pole barn. (I never saw it, but apparently it dispatched the turkeys quickly by them being placed head down in a sort of cone whereon their throats were swiftly cut). There was the noise of all the chatter of the pluckers. Somewhere in the corner of the room Ken Bruce was playing Popmaster or it could have been Radio Devon, you couldn't really make it out. A Labrador puppy was running around throwing feathers into the air and sniffing the dead birds' beaks. Children of all ages were coming in and out of the room (the farmer's kids all get the day off school to help with the turkey plucking) and some fairly young ones were working away with the smaller turkeys on their laps. Someone had just brought in a tray of tea and a tin of biscuits was being passed round, the pluckers barely stopping to wipe their hands on boiler suit trousers far less pristine than mine, before taking a biscuit. It was incredibly atmospheric. It spoke of community and long-forgotten ways in which we all used to live. I loved it.

We were shown to a space on the benches and

Lorna's cousins all shifted a bit to make room for us. A dead, but still warm turkey was placed on my lap, and we were off. As inappropriate jokes about me being a turkey plucker's wife raced through my head, I grabbed hold of a bunch of feathers and pulled hard. As they came out, the turkey took his head off my knees, looked me straight in the eye and said "Oww! That hurt!" Of course, he didn't. But I expected them to every time.

Turkey plucking is hard work. Getting the wing feathers out is the hardest and requires pliers and a hard tug. It needs effort. It's easy to see how these sorts of feathers would have been used as writing instruments in days gone by. The quills are strong and thick and feel robost enough to write with. The rest of the feathers come out easier but there are an awful lot of them. You have to keep your thumb and forefinger pinched and pull the feathers swiftly upwards for hours on end as you pluck bird after bird after bird. It is repetitive and there is a certain end of the bird (I'll leave it to you imagination) where the work gets pretty mucky. Pooey turkeys indeed. Right in your lap, right on your cold and aching fingers. It's their last act of revenge. The birds have to be plucked whilst they are still warm as it's easier to get the feathers out, and after a while I began to be quite grateful for the warmth of the bird on my lap. It was the middle of December after all, and there was a slight drifting of snow falling outside. It was beginning to look a lot like Christmas.

Lorna's cousins did all they could to make the two novices in the clean boiler suits welcome. They tried to engage us in conversation. Unfortunately, I hadn't really learned to speak Devonian at the time and I could hardly make out a word. "Where you be fram?" was a good starter. "Oh, we are at Spillers Farm in Musbury," I replied. "'Eee be (mumble, mumble, indistinct words, was Ken Bruce doing the three in ten there? gobble, gobble, mumble) reet be tha men red a Spillers oi by Edward's?" Having no idea what had just been said I nodded and smiled in return, wiped my aching hand on my dirty boiler suit leg and took a biscuit from the proffered tin.

After a spectacular hot two course lunch during which everyone ate a great deal, we returned to work. Nobody seemed to be on the Keto diet, or counting calories, or be allergic to anything. They all tucked in to platefuls of steaming hot cottage pie followed by crumble and custard, with great gusto. I have immense respect for farmers. They are wonderful people. Hard working hardly seems a worthy way to describe them. They are strong, no-nonsense types who get on with the job in hand no matter how tiring or hard it might be. They are real.

By the end of the day I was knackered. No, not just knackered. Cold too. Cold and knackered. Despite the fact that I'd been wearing a thermal vest, thermal long-johns, at least three layers and the (by now, filthy and feathery) boiler suit, I was freezing. Sitting fairly immobile for hours on end on a bench in a stone building in December, one can start to feel the temperature. After a long hot bath and a good sleep, we were up and at it again the next day.

Towards the end of the second day the 'Killing Machine' fell quiet and the gobbling stopped. What a relief! I was not only grateful for the relative quiet, but the fact that soon my cramping fingers would be able to move from the permanent plucking posture they had been in for the past 48 hours, and I could straighten my aching back and get the feeling back in my frozen feet.

I don't know who plucked our turkeys. Maybe us, maybe one of the kids, maybe one of Lorna's cousins, but in all the hundreds that had been plucked someone had been keeping track of ours, and they were all hanging on a rail waiting for us to take them home.

After plucking, a turkey requires hanging for a few days to develop flavour. The bird still needs to be intact for this. All its innards are secure and it's still got its head and feet. It's just naked. Not having a secure barn where we could be sure they wouldn't be eaten by a passing fox (which really would have rankled after all that freezing hard work), we hung them in the holiday cottage. This can be a dodgy time for the turkeys. They need to be killed a couple of weeks prior to eating to ensure there is time for plucking, hanging and drawing. But they also need to be kept cold. If the weather is warm they will start to deteriorate too fast. Fortunately, it was absolutely freezing the year we had turkeys. Proper snow, ice on the lake, we didn't have to worry. Until we got to the drawing stage.

Because, dear reader, the cold, freezing, yucky hard work isn't over yet. After hanging for a few days comes the drawing. Brace yourself. You cut the head, neck and feet off. Take the skin off the neck, put it to one side. Put your hand into the hole where the neck once was and push against the rib cage, keeping the back of your hand along the ribs and keep pushing until most of the lower part of your arm (depending on the size of the turkey) is inside the bird. Eventually you'll get to the end of the bird and now you turn your hand to cup whatever it is you've got your hand on and pull. It's like turning a turkey inside out as the insides of the bird come out through where its neck used to be. Try to ignore the lacerations on the back of your hand from the sharp rib cage as you pull. Most of it gets discarded but now is time to separate the (surprisingly small) heart and liver and set aside with the neck and find the gizzard. Find the what? Hmmm, yes, the gizzard. Don't ask me what it is, or what it does but it belongs with the other bits and bobs that you've put aside that make up the giblets. (According to Wikipedia, the gizzard is a specialised part of the stomach in certain animals – birds in particular – and it is used to grind up food).

There is a very particular way to cut the gizzard as you have to discard one part of it (possibly the spleen, potentially the gall bladder) but keep the rest, and if you puncture the part you need to discard it stinks. Really stinks. After all, that bird's last meal was weeks ago now. You only make that mistake once.

Anyway, put the gizzard with the other giblets, put them in a plastic bag and shove them back into the cold bird, tie up its legs and wings and pop it in a box for a happy customer to come and collect on Christmas Eve. And do the next one. Did I mention we were doing this in the freezing cold? By the time we were on the last bird I had lost the feeling in my fingers and could barely pick up a knife to cut the gizzard, let alone cut the right bit. Fortunately, the cold meant I could no longer feel the backs of my hands which looked like they were dying the death of a thousand cuts.

The next day the customers came to pick up their turkeys. Happily chatting about Christmas and all the joy it brings we handed over their dinnertime centrepieces for what I had considered to be quite a lot of money before I'd had to process the turkeys. Now I didn't think it was half enough.

We never had turkeys of our own on the farm again but returned year after year to Lorna's to join in the plucking. We would do a day or two of plucking in return for a turkey for our Christmas dinner. Lorna no longer farms turkeys. This past Christmas I asked Sarah (Lorna's daughter), once my neighbour at Spillers and now my friend and hairdresser, if she knew anyone who was doing turkeys, she gave me the name of someone at a farm near to where we now live. When I arrived to collect the turkey, they were all being handed out from a small stone room next to a large warehouse-sized pole barn. Knowing full well that they would no doubt be related or at least know her I mentioned that I used to pluck turkeys for Lorna. "Oh Aunty Lorna", came the reply. "She's my dad's cousin".

SWANS

The turkeys were almost the largest birds we had at
Spillers. They were surpassed only by the swans.
We didn't farm the swans of course. For a start
they all used to belong to the Queen, but I suspect
she passed them on along with the crown, sceptre

and all that jazz. But swans were a definite feature of life at Spillers. There seemed to be a lot of swans around the Axe Valley area. The Axe was the river that cut the valley in which Spillers sat. Maybe that was what made it so beautiful.

Spillers sat in an official Area of Outstanding Beauty just into the Devon border. And it was (and still is) absolutely beautiful. Situated between two hills, one hill behind us and one in front, it was incredibly picturesque, with a lovely, gently flowing river winding its way between fields towards the nearby coast at Axmouth where it joined the sea. It was lovely in all weathers, but on a sunny day it really was outstanding, and well deserved its moniker. I used to walk along the river as often as possible. Crossing a small ditch at the back of what we called 'the lake field', I would trespass onto Edward's land (not really trespassing, him and all his family knew I did it. I don't think they minded) and walk through one of his fields to the river.

The first time I ventured down that way was to check out what I thought was an old farm worker's cottage at the riverbank. Looking from our bedroom window, I could see a small, stone structure with two squares for what I presumed had been windows and a rectangular shape for a door. It had a grass roof. Not in the way that a progressive borough council had deliberately turfed a building to boost their green credentials, I mean the kind of grass roof you get with the passage of time and neglect. I really needed to see what it was.

So, after we had been at Spillers for a few weeks I trespassed my way down there to check it out. It certainly wasn't a farm workers' cottage. Any farm worker given that as a home would wonder what they'd done wrong. It was a totally concrete structure with a large block in the middle, the idea being (Keith later explained to me) that if a gun was fired into it, the bullet would ricochet back onto the shooter. It was a pillbox, and it formed part of the Taunton Stop Line. The Taunton Stop Line was one of more than fifty similar defensive lines constructed during World War II. It ran from Seaton in Devon, along the River Axe and continued into Somerset with plenty of fortifications along rural railway lines and the Bridgwater and Taunton canal, until it reached the north coast of Somerset. The fortifications were designed to stop the enemy should Hitler have ever decided to invade Devon, an idea which seemed faintly ridiculous to me in the early 2000's but would have seemed a real and frightening prospect in the 1940's. This was the same reason for which the rural road signs were removed and never replaced, which made our trips to drop Cassie at her boyfriend's such a trauma. When we visited Seaton we saw much more complicated fortifications, including a really large pillbox staring blankly out to sea waiting for Mr Hitler. I never failed to think of Dad's Army every time I looked at that 'workers cottage' after that.

I was never really alone in my venturings. Our beautiful dog Merryck would always be with me. Whatever the weather we would escape every day just to get into the valley. Wandering along by the river I once was lucky enough to see an otter, lying on its back paws clasped to its chest, in the classic 'otter relaxing' pose, before it caught sight of me and disappeared under the water. I was quite enamoured with seeing the otter, until one harsh winter when we realised it had probably eaten all the fish in our lake. Still, it had to survive one way or another. It might have been beautiful, but it was still an otter eat fish world.

During the summer the fields would be full of cows, including Edward's field behind us. I was scared of cows for the first seven years we lived at Spillers. I was terrified of the size of them, their heavy breathing and the way they stared at you with that 'You want some? I'll give you some', look in their eye. I was so scared of them that I would either try to time the walks to get out and back to Spillers before they reached that particular field, or I would walk in another direction deliberately. Often was the time when I mistimed it and got stuck behind a gate leading into Edward's field and my fear would stop me going any further. I would phone Keith and ask him to come and get me and escort me and Merryck (who was also pretty scared of cows) back home. One day I realised I was walking through the cows without fear. "Well, there's a thing", I said to myself. "I'm no longer scared of cows." It only took seven years.

But the other feature of these walks was the swans. In the winter, the fields were emptier. Occasionally there'd be a flock of sheep, but often the fields would be dotted with other large white creatures. Swans, in pairs, small groups, or enough for a lamentation would be feeding on the moist grass with their elegant, long necks dipping and rising. There was a nearby swannery at Abbotsbury (worth a visit), and possibly these swans were on their way to or from there, but there were also a few who nested on the river, and closer to home, on the island in the middle of our lake.

Our journey with the swans at Spillers started with tragedy. We had a telegraph pole in the lake field, part of a string of them over the nearby fields carrying electricity to the local villages. Here is an interesting fact. What is the most common cause of death among swans? Sadly, it is electrocution. As swans come into land and settle for the evening, they tend to by flying in the dusk and heading towards water. Electric wires are hard for swans to see at dusk and often they will fly into the wires and electrocute themselves. This happened with the first swans we ever saw at Spillers. We woke one morning to see a dead swan lying by the lake with its mate next to it. Swans mate for life and so this poor swan had just lost its soulmate. That swan sat by the dead body all day, until eventually flying away the following evening. It was one of the saddest things I have ever seen.

If you see a dead swan you have to report it to DEFRA, which we duly did, and after a while they came and took away the body, which by then had been nibbled a bit by passing foxes. I think maybe they were the ones to tell us about the electrocution, so we contacted the utility company responsible for the telegraph pole. They came along and hung little circular disks on the wires, making them more visible for descending swans who can then take aversive action and land safely. So, if you see those little circles hanging from wires whilst out in the countryside, now you know why they're there.

Once swans had started to land safely on the water, they arrived every year. And they nested every year. I assume it was the same pair, but they would arrive sometime in January or February. The sound of swans flying overhead is quite something. Actually, it's not really the sound of them flying; from the middle of the lake field it was more the sound of them descending and landing. It's quite majestic. Their wings are huge and it's hard to describe the enormous, swooping sound of two pairs of wings sweeping and swooping up and down in tandem. As they get really near the water, they stick their big paddle feet out and touch down, curving their wings inwards to slow themselves to a stop before folding their majestic wings back in and giving a little shake of their tail feather to settle everything back in place. It's an incredible and graceful movement for such a large bird. Watching them take off is even more awe-inspiring, as it never looked like there was enough space – but they always made it. They'd get some forward motion by running hell for leather with their necks at full stretch on the water with their wings outstretched, before opening some invisible throttle and flapping those amazing wings which provided enough lift to get them airborne, then they just have to keep flapping in huge, swooping movements. If there were any Canada geese around (and there often were), there would be a bit of a stand-off, which the swans would inevitably win (size matters). The geese would fly off to nest elsewhere, and the female swan would start making a nest.

The nests were majestic, large creations and were well-tended. Once the eggs were laid, the swans took it in turn to sit on the nest in all weathers. It could be absolutely pouring, but the swan would sit there, sometimes with its head under its wing for a little shelter. Whilst one was sitting the other would be on guard in the water or feeding. I could only marvel at their tenacity. We would usually visit the lake daily just for five minutes and often play with our dog up there, but when the swans were nesting we gave them room. For start, the male had this way of throwing his fantastic wings over his back and advancing in waves in quite a threatening manner whilst fixing us with a stare that said: "It could be an urban myth, but apparently I can break a man's arm. Not sure how I do it, but I'm willing to let you find out if you come any closer."

We all came close to finding out whether a swan can break your arm one year when Mrs Swan had been off the nest feeding for a while and for the first time in years, collided with the Stillduck. Getting herself in a complete flap, she managed to wrap the long cord and weight around her leg making it difficult for her to move, let alone get back on the nest. This all happened on an Easter Sunday. Keith and I started phoning aound for a Swanherd (yes, it's an actual thing), but there aren't many around, especially on an Easter Sunday. Eventually, a lovely man called Dudley from the RSPCA turned up with a long pole and a net. The plan was to set her free whilst distracting Mr Swan at the same time. Mrs Swan had managed to get herself back on the nest with the Stillduck strapped to her leg. Keith and Dudly rowed to the island. Dudley got out of the boat and.... DIVED.... and managed to catch Mrs Swan. He cut her free, and Keith and he rowed back to shore before the potential-arm-breaker had even seen them. The Stillduck remained sitting on the bank watching the swans from a safe distance.

It normally took a couple of months but around late April each month we would be able to spot little fluffy bundles of grey peeping out from the nest, or being carried around on the mother's back like one of those odd little pontoon boats you see on some lakes. It was wonderful watching them teach their cygnets to feed. The adults dipping their glorious necks down into the water to fetch some pond weed and watching the little grey cygnets try to do the same but be prevented by their own buoyancy. They'd just keep bobbing up again. It was hilarious. But they soon got the hang of it.

Which is more than can be said for their parents. I don't know if it was because they were juveniles themselves and didn't really know what they were doing, or because by May time Spillers was getting busier and this disturbed them, or because they are just crap parents, but inevitably year after year about three weeks after the cygnets hatched, the adult swans just flew off. They'd just leave, as if to say: "Stuff this for a game of soldiers. I've had enough of this parenting lark. Let's go to Lanzarote for the week" and they were never seen again. Until the next January. This always left us with quite the dilemma. There were little cygnets out there for whom we now somehow felt responsible. The first couple of years we tried rescue. We took the boat out to the nest and tried to get the cygnets to follow us. Having read the story of the ducklings earlier you can imagine how well that worked out. We managed it one year and took them to live with some ducklings we had hatched. However, within 48 hours they were all dead. We rang the nearby swannery who told us that no matter what we did, it was unlikely to be successful as they would probably have died of stress anyway.

However, it at least meant that we got the lake back which was good for our B&B and cottage guests. I'm not sure having an aggressive and territorial male swan on the lake with growing young would have worked out, so maybe it was for the best. We saw other nesting swans on the River Axe with a brood that they raised to adulthood, so perhaps it was just the wrong place for them and it took a few years for them to realise that.

We did have the most amazing experience with the swans. One February afternoon, Keith and I were just taking a bit of time out at the lake. We had put benches up there and we were sitting on one of these gazing at a pair of swans on the water right in front of us. I don't know what made us both realise, something about the way they were swimming near each other mirroring each other's movement, but I said to him, "I think they're going to do a mating dance", and sure enough that's exactly what they did. They entwined their necks, they made their necks into the shape of a heart, they raised themselves up on their paddling feet heads up, wings stretched right out and balanced there perfectly for a few seconds in perfect symmetry. It was absolutely breath-taking, and I knew that if I stopped looking for one second it would be over. I was berating myself for having left my phone in the house, far too far to fetch and still see them doing this show stopping performance. So instead, I just decided to live in the moment and take it all in. I couldn't believe it. It wasn't as if it was on the other side of the lake. It was literally right in front of our eyes. It was one of the highlights of my life and it was incredibly special. All that was lacking was David Attenborough doing the voiceover. They might be crap parents, but they're incredible dancers.

SILS AND THE STER

I have mentioned them in passing, but now is time to fill you in more fully on our Pest Control Officers, Sils and The Ster. After we had been at Spillers for a couple of months, Edward came over to pawn off two kittens from his cat's latest litter. This may have been the first time we met him and he obviously thought two recently-arrived Londoners were ripe for taking a couple of kittens off his hands. He had the most amazing cat. Martha was pretty old even when we heard of her. She was a typical farm cat. Very much the outdoor type, she rarely came into their house and had by then had about 14 litters or something ludicrous, so more kittens were definitely not what Edward wanted. Telling us they were the last two left, he persuaded us (and when I say us, I mean Keith), that a farm really needed a couple of cats around to keep down the rodent population etc. As we were to discover, they brought in more mice than they killed, playing with them in the kitchen then getting bored and wandering off to leave us to catch the terrified creatures and return them to the wild. However, I did also get used to the sight of a perfectly dissected stomach sitting on the kitchen mat. They might eat the mouse, but they would not eat whatever the mouse had eaten. That was below them.

Naming them after a couple of my recent bosses, we called them Nicky and Sila (pronounced Cilla). They were black and white (the cats, not the bosses), with four white paws each. Sila had a strip of white on her nose and Nicky had a single white spot on the end of his. We should have called him Domino. In fact, as he grew (and he grew quite a lot – a vet once described him as "at the top end" of the feline BMI scale) I did occasionally call him Fats Domino. Sila had the loudest purr in the world, you could hear it in the room next door. Nicky was a silent purrer. The only way to know he was purring was to touch him and feel the vibrations.

They were a formidable hunting team. I used to watch them casually strolling around the field as if they were lions on the Savannah. And I still have a mental image of them sitting either side of a molehill, both staring at the mound, almost daring the mole to appear. It was as if they were saying: "Any time, pal, any time. I've got all day. I literally don't have anything else to do."

Then there was the time that they brought a magpie into the tearoom. The tearoom was two storeys at the time and one morning before we had too much B&B business (fortunately), there was a terrible racket from the upper storey. I went up to find the animal equivalent of the final scene from Reservoir Dogs - cups and saucers in disarray, some crockery broken, bird poo on the floor and tables, a battered and defeated-looking magpie hanging by one leg from the radiator and Sils and The Ster staring up at him and looking mighty pleased with themselves. I had no idea what had happened, but once again, it was up to us to grab their victim and release him back into the wild, whilst trying to avoid being pecked in the face for our trouble. We also once adopted a baby swallow that Sila had captured. We took it from her jaws and called it Throat. We tried to keep it alive by feeding it on hen food, but alas, it died. If we'd fed it on worms and bugs it may have had more of a chance, but we were obviously a bit clueless.

The cats loved the heat of the AGA. They loved it

so much, that I would often open the cupboard next to the permanently hot cooker and reach to the back looking for one my largest saucepans, only to be greeted by four green eyes steadily staring back at me as if to say: "Do you mind? You're causing an awful draught" At some point in the afternoon there would be a shifting of pans and a sort of knocking and they would emerge one after the other, stretch and head out to the Savannah. I don't really know how they got in there. It was a bespoke, built-in cupboard sort of kitchen and that door wasn't a perfect fit. Obviously no match for a determined paw. I never really knew when they were in there and I used to pray that they wouldn't emerge when the Environmental Health Officer was visiting. Sila was a real lap cat and once tried to sit on the EHO's lap during one visit. I grabbed her and shooed her out the back door, with a "who's cat is that?!" sort of gesture and hoped that the EHO was a cat person and wouldn't close us down. I think she must have written "Must try harder" on her report.

Sila also wanted to travel. She could not resist an open car door, and if the postie or a delivery man arrived leaving the engine running and the door open, in she would pop and settle herself down in the footwell ready for adventure. I dreaded the day she would do it to one of the guests. I could just imagine them arriving home after a four-hour journey for Sils to jump out of the car and start cleaning herself with them staring at each other and asking themselves who packed a cat.

I suppose I should clear up Nicky's name change. Their names were a bit of a joke. The eponymous married couple after whom they were named were two lovely people, but Nicky never really suited our cat as a name. So, we started to call him Nickster. Then Mr Nickster. Then The Nickster, until finally dispensing with Nicky altogether and settling on The Ster. It was never Ster. He always had the full moniker. We always used the definite article. He was always The Ster. And that suited him. He was a cat of great character and thought very highly of himself. He would always announce his arrival when he walked into a room drawing attention to himself with a single "Mew", as if to say: "I'm here."

Once again, the animal hierarchy was in evidence with our cats. Sila would do all the work to catch some prey, a mouse or a shrew. She would be teasing and playing with it. The Ster would walk into the room, stroll over to her and she would immediately drop it and let him take over. He would do the killing and eating and then she would groom him. Female emancipation never made it to the animal kingdom.

However, it was Sila who did the most amazing thing I've ever seen in a cat. One slightly sunny winter afternoon Keith and I were sitting at the lake. We had been joined by our lovely dog Merryck and

The Ster. Sila was obviously feeling a bit left out and so came strolling across the field until she was directly opposite the bench on which we all sat (Ster vibrating on my lap). She started to walk one way, then turned and walked the other and back again. I said to Keith, "She's trying to work out the quickest way to get to us, but she won't swim across because cats hate the water." And with those words barely out of my mouth, Sila jumped into the water! She did about three or four strokes of doggy paddle before realising she was a cat and turned and headed back to the shore. By now the rest of her family had leapt up from the bench and started to run around the lake towards her. Dragging herself back onto the bank just as we reached her, we all headed back into the house, with a very bedraggled Sils trying to shake the water from her fur all the way back through the field. I didn't know whether to laugh or applaud. I laughed of course.

Many were the days when I would open the lounge curtains to see The Ster staring back at me from the hedge on the opposite side of the road. The road was a double-edged sword for Spillers. The house was built right on the busy A358, the road between Axminster and Seaton, just past the bend that marked the edge of the village of Musbury and just before a straight stretch of road that many drivers imagined was an invitation to pretend that they were Lewis Hamilton and had just been given the chequered flag. Of course, when the house was built sometime in the 1850's, its proximity to the road would have been an advantage, and the traffic - such as it was - would have gone clip, clop, clip, clop. It was of some advantage to us as it attracted passing trade and besides, all the true beauty of Spillers was out the back in the other direction. However, in our time there we saw a number of accidents. We saw the Devon Air Ambulance pick up at least two poor souls and had the small wall outside the house knocked down twice. On one occasion we woke up in the morning to find the wall in pieces in our garden with no idea what had happened. A builder soon came along to fix the wall and told us the story. Apparently two young lads had been travelling in separate cars back from a night out at Seaton with another car in between them at about two in the morning. Seeing the bend too late, the driver of the first car had lost control and hit our wall, causing the second car to crash into his and the third crash into the second. All the drivers were not hurt and so congregated by the first car and the conversation went something like this:

Driver 3 (friend of Driver 1) "Are you OK mate?"

Driver 1 "Yeah, I think so."

Driver 3 "Your mum's going to be livid that you've wrecked her car. Better not tell her you'd been drinking"

Driver 2 "It's worse than that son. I'm an off-duty

Police Officer. You're nicked!"

So, I was often understandably nervous seeing The Ster staring silently back at me from the hedge. Sila never crossed the road. She had the smarts. Not The Ster. He was a wonderfully laid-back sort of creature. Incredibly lazy, he had a very casual approach to life and I remember thinking that he would be the kind of cat that would live into his 20's, relaxing his way to old age.

Sadly, it was not to be. He only made it to three years old. Heading out to feed the hens early one morning Keith started running towards the road. Immediately I knew what had happened. He picked up The Ster's body from the grass verge where it had been thrown. He was still warm but I'm sure he died instantly and literally would not have known what hit him. Later that day we took his body to the island on the middle of the lake and buried him.

I don't know if Sila missed her brother, but without him around she started to follow us all the time. She took to coming for a walk with us whenever we walked Merryck. Sometimes she'd give up when we were just a few hundred yards from home, but once she persisted. About halfway around the walk she'd had enough and set up an insistent mewing that told us she was fed up. After half an hour or so of this infernal noise I told Keith I was going to take her home. Realising that she'd have no idea where she was by now, I decided I'd have to carry her. I knew Sila was not going to enjoy this. She hated being picked up. But with no choice, I bent down and picked up the reluctant mewing machine and turned back for home, only to have her squirm and mew in my face all the way back. After that walking the dog became a covert operation. If Sila was in the vicinity as we set off down the lane that marked the start of the walk we would yell to each other; "Leg it! Here comes the cat!" and we would try to outrun her. Often we succeeded and after a while she gave up the idea, preferring to pretend to ignore us as we crept past her on our way out.

After we'd been at Spillers for a few years we decided to open a farm shop. Not one of the faux supermarkets that you see nowadays, that sell everything from galoshes to olive oil at ridiculously inflated prices, but a much smaller affair. It was literally a shop on a farm. It was a way to sell some of our spare produce with some extras. Any way we could think of to turn one pound into two and help chip away at some of that massive mortgage.

One day I was hanging around behind the counter hoping the lone customer would buy something, anything, when she said; "Is she sleeping there because her name is Mushroom?" "What?", I replied wondering what on earth she was talking about, until I followed her gaze to see Sila curled up in a tight, unconscious ball in an empty basket that was labelled "Mushrooms", next to other baskets labelled "Courgettes" and "Cauliflowers". "Yes.

She's always nagging us to add the possessive apostrophe," I managed not to say.

THE FARM SHOP

You would think that a flourishing tearoom, B&B business, holiday cottage, caravan site and working smallholding would have been enough to keep us busy. And busy was the word. I have no idea how many steps we walked each day, but I would imagine 10,000 would have been completed by about 9am leaving the rest of the day free to complete the equivalent of walking to John O' Groats and back. However, we were now in the credit crunch of 2008, which had a dramatic effect on the tearoom business. Whereas people had thought nothing of coming in their droves and ordering 10 cream teas, now you'd find groups of families ordering a pot of tea for four and three extra cups and saucers. However, our mortgage still remained nice and fat, so with one narrowing revenue stream we had to find another. Hence, a farm shop. And that's how we found ourselves balancing a large open drinks dispenser cabinet in the back of our trailer along the fast-moving A3052 from Exeter.

We'd obviously not learned anything from the free gift of the Soay. Having seen an advert for a drinks' cabinet going free to a good home in the nearby city of Exeter, we set off with the trailer to fetch it. Much larger than we had reckoned for, we loaded it onto the trailer and tied it down as best we could with several bits of rope. We couldn't believe our luck, that someone was giving away a drinks' cabinet. After we had driven home very slowly watching it wobble away in the back, and plugged it in, we knew why they were giving it away. It hummed quite loudly and gave out an occasional shudder as if the whole thing was shutting down. However, we loaded it with our spare produce and hoped it would encourage more business.

The farm shop wasn't our most successful venture. Often people would walk in, look around and ask us "Where's the farm shop?", seeming a bit confused and vacant when we told them they were in it. We were hampered a little by the fact that there was a much larger and extremely well-stocked farm shop just down the road which went by the name of Millers. Customers expecting there to be shelves of marinated olives and handmade candles were often disappointed by our display of home grown veg and handmade pies. It also meant that I spent my days behind the counter waiting on the occasional customer instead of in my natural habitat of the kitchen.

I loved being in the kitchen, hiding away from it all. Keith was a natural front man, and very good at it he was too. Keith has a real gift of the gab and was very good at making B&B guests feel relaxed. His main ability was to get two tables of guests to start talking and then withdraw, leaving us to have a few minutes of peace in the kitchen. He would regale the guests with all our tales (much as I'm doing with you now), his favourite topic being the pigs and his favourite line being "there's no money in pigs". If I had a pound for every time I heard that I could have paid off the mortgage that hung like an albatross around our necks.

One of my favourite memories of overhearing Keith in the tearoom whilst I was in the kitchen came in the quite early days. At the time, Keith bore a passing resemblance to Richard Gere and used to love it when anyone else noticed. But after a few years working his fingers to the bone and me cutting, or rather shearing, his hair into a crew cut the resemblance had faded. A group of women came in and whilst settling down one of them turned to Keith and said, "You remind me of somebody." I could hear Keith puffing himself up ready for the compliment of being compared to a Hollywood heartthrob when he said, "I know. It's Richard Gere isn't it?" "No, no, not Richard Gere," came the bemused reply. "It's Jim Bowen." It's a long fall from the star of Pretty Woman to the star of Sunday teatime darts show Bullseye. Alongside the sound of Keith's ego rapidly deflating, was me in the kitchen laughing until the tears ran down my legs

RIVER COTTAGE

"You guys should come and have a look at what they're doing to Park Farm" said Rudi in early 2007. Rudi and Lyn had become pretty much our only link to the outside world since they came to clear the lake of weed in our first summer. They had dredged the lake using a ladder, the weed clumping around the rungs which they removed before dragging the ladder back through the water to remove more. Rudi was a keen fisherman who lived in the nearby village and knew a fair amount about water management. After dredging the lake, he then stocked it with various fish (which were unfortunately eaten by my friend the otter in a particularly cold winter a couple of years later. We would trudge through the snow every day to find another fish head on the edge of the lake.) Once stocked, Rudi procured a couple of hay bales which were suspended in the corners of the lake. He told us this would prevent more weed building up. He was right. He knew all sorts of things, including what was happening at Park Farm.

Park Farm was directly opposite Spillers as the crow flies, if the crow flew over the hill opposite us and into the valley beyond. We'd never heard of it but joined him and Lyn as we drove out one Sunday afternoon to have a look. Turning off a road and descending a very steep and stone-laden path we soon saw a large farmhouse at the bottom. It had been gutted and there was obviously a lot of building work in progress. A couple of men – builders, we presumed – emerged from the house just as we arrived outside and we beat as hasty a retreat as you can make whist performing an 18-point turn and heading back up a stone strewn narrow path.

"What's going on there then?" I asked. "Some celebrity chef has bought it," answered Rudi. Soon rumours began to spread that the celebrity chef in question was High Fernley-Whittingstall. Campaigner, chef, foody and all-round good guy Hugh. Of all the villages in all the world, he chose to move into ours. And it changed our lives.

Once Park Farm had been turned into River Cottage HQ we never had to tout for business again.

TRIP ADVISOR

River Cottage HQ changed everything. Being close neighbours, we got to know the people working at the office at HQ and got ourselves on the accommodation list. But we were not alone. The world and his wife and dog were straining to get on that list. Anyone who had a cupboard to let within a 20-mile radius was on that list and – of course – the list was in alphabetical order, which put us a long way down from the top. But, bless their hearts, if you rang the people in the office and asked where to stay, they always suggested Spillers. We were actively doing what they were filming. They were pretending to be a smallholding; we were actually living it.

And the business flourished. From the moment River Cottage opened its doors we were always full. The impact was immediate. The power of television was evident. Hoardes of people – Londoners mainly – descended on our little corner of paradise every weekend and they packed out all the available accommodation for miles around. They came to experience 'the good life', they came to meet Hugh, they came to see River Cottage. We visited River Cottage several times and it was transformed from the hollow shell that we had seen into a stylish and classy farm-like film set. The early days of River Cottage were the best. Hugh was there often and was very hands-on and involved, doing cookery demonstrations, signing books, teaching people about sustainable and seasonal eating. The food at River Cottage HQ was always good and it had a lovely friendly atmosphere. River Cottage HQ and the subsequent River Cottage Canteen in Axminster brought thousands of visitors to the area. I'm sure it all changed the local economy. The taxi firms had more work than they could handle, the B&Bs were all full and it was all because of a chef who really cared about food and its environmental impact.

It was all absolutely brilliant, until the creation of

Trip Advisor. Trip Advisor came to terrify me. It was like having the Sword of Damocles constantly hanging over your head. Unless everything was absolutely perfect you could never be sure of what sort of review you'd get, and not everything can be perfect all the time. An overwhelming majority of our reviews were brilliant, kind and of the five-star variety, but there were those who complained about the smallest, most trivial things, such as not liking the colour of the paint on our walls. A strange thing to say about a room in which you've got your eyes closed most of the time.

We had a couple of near misses too, which could have led to some awful reviews. There was the power cut, brought on by our neighbours trimming the hedges on the road and cutting through our power line at the same time. We had to barbeque the breakfast next morning. Barbequed bacon doesn't work. Or like the time that the ceiling fell in just after the guests had finished breakfast. As the tearoom business started to decline and the B&B business increased, we (I say we, I mean Keith) had converted the top floor of the tearoom into an extra en-suite bedroom. After a few years, the shower started leaking one day and within a few hours an ominous bump appeared in the tearoom ceiling. Breakfast that morning was a pretty rushed affair. With one eye on the bump, the usual chat about there being no money in pigs was cut pretty short as we tried to get guests out of the door before the bump got bigger. We just about had them all out before

CRASH!

the ceiling was all over the breakfast dishes. The
good thing about Keith is, that whilst his plumbing
skills leave a lot to be desired, he can turn his hand
to anything and the ceiling was sorted before the
end of the day. That is also something that people
don't realise about this dream of a lifestyle. Unless
you are prepared to cope with sudden disaster and
can fix it yourself, don't bother. You can't wait for
someone else to come round and sort it.

Talking of Keith's plumbing skills, there was also
that time water was pouring through the ceiling.
We'd been renovating one of the bathrooms and
late in the afternoon a drip started in our lounge
which was under the main en-suite room. I was
monitoring the drip with a bucket, whilst Keith and
our decorator Paul, tried to fix it. I don't know what
they did, but instead of one drip, there suddenly
appeared three or four. I was frantically placing
and emptying buckets when the doorbell rang. An
expected guest stood at the front door. Ushering
her in and trying not to look too panicked I
explained that I was dealing with a bit of a
'situation', and she came to the doorway of our
lounge to behold what was now a cascade of water
flowing from the ceiling above. "Is it alright if I have
a bath?" she confusingly asked. I looked round at
her, bucket in hand, and very nearly said, "Sure you

wouldn't rather have a shower love? You could just stand under this lot."

At first the B&B was all a novelty. I'm naturally an introvert and would happily spend the whole day alone not really talking to anybody. I'm married to a natural extrovert, so Keith was very much in charge of the chat. But running the B&B gave me the ability to talk to anyone, about anything. I am now an expert in small talk. I could enter a small talk championship. But I'm not sure that having such constant shallow conversations is good for anyone. Having no conversation of any depth for months on end makes you feel like you're shrivelling inside. No wonder the late Queen was so tiny. A life of constant small talk, I'm surprised she hadn't disappeared altogether. I shall watch Charles 3 for signs of shrinkage.

It's a very odd profession being a B&B owner. There's a certain intimacy having strangers sleeping in your house. You hear them snoring, laughing, coughing, watching telly and doing other much more intimate things which I will leave to your imaginations, and then you make them breakfast. After they've left you clean up after them. Some people leave the room like it's a small earthquake, with others you wouldn't even know they'd been there. You have to strip the sometimes stained bedding, pick up random bits of clothing that have been left, wipe pubic hairs from the shower, flush unmentionables down the toilet, polish, hoover, scrub, remake the beds with freshly ironed bedding, empty bins, replace the herbal tea bags etc (because everyone takes them even though you know they won't ever use them) and generally make the room look like nobody has ever been in it before. And then people complain because they don't like the colour of the paint on the walls. You tell people the room will be ready at 3pm and they turn up at 11am. You ask people not to flush things down the toilet that will block up our septic tank and they take no notice. We regularly had to pull sanitary products out of the septic tank (when I saw we, I mean Keith).

We saw such a plethora of people that it was occasionally hard to keep track. We had four letting bedrooms and they were all full in the seasonal months, and we took people in for one night, which many B&Bs don't. This meant that for at least eight months of the year there was a potential turnover of 28 different couples each week. The off-season was also fairly busy, meaning that we never had a weekend without somebody staying with us. This was an incredible blessing, but it also meant a great deal of small talk and an element of face blindness. After a few years of living that way, you have no idea how many faces you've actually seen. Making small talk with one couple from Denmark one Sunday morning, as they were due to leave, I asked them if it was the first time they'd been to England. She looked at me a little askance and said: "It's not even the first time we've been to Spillers".

DAY TO DAY LIFE

I want to try and help you feel how it felt to live that life. How it was so dark in the winter it felt like being surrounded by inky, black velvet. We were half a mile from the village, so there were no pavements, no street lighting, no light pollution at all. In the winter it was dark. A darkness so thick that it almost wraps itself around you like a blanket. A darkness that only country people know. I used to hate getting things from the freezers in the winter. The freezers were in the garage that was across the yard. It was only a matter of a few hundred feet but coming from the city I had never really experienced darkness like that, and I was always a bit on edge. It was darkness so black you could feel it, and I used to count the steps until I felt for the garage door handle and once inside feel for the light switch. The fluorescent light bulbs would blink on and off a couple of times before finally banishing the darkness with their garish light. Then, having retrieved whatever it was I wanted, I'd have to flick it back off and do the terrifying return journey! I'm so at home with the dark now that I can't sleep if there's a street light within half a mile.

Some clear nights were better than other because the winter skies were full of stars. Incredibly full, like an invisible hand had taken a pocket full of diamonds and flung them across the inky, blackness of the velvet and I was quite mesmerised by them. So mesmerised that we bought a telescope, determined to teach ourselves the names of the stars and constellations, and be able to view the rings of Saturn. Unfortunately, most of our star gazing had to be done in the winter and that's a pretty damn cold hobby. Particularly if you're doing it though a telescope with dodgy Chinese instructions that you don't really understand. So, after a couple of freezing nights not looking at much in particular, we took the telescope back indoors to our bedroom. And after a lot of looking at the moon ("just point it at the biggest, shiniest thing in the sky"), the telescope just became something else to dust.

Winter sunsets were stunning. As the sun was so low in the sky it would throw amazing, deeply red and purple colours into the clouds that would resemble a Turner artwork spread out across the sky towards the coast at Seaton.

In the summer months it was the opposite. Having no immediate neighbours and nothing to mar our view, the sun seemed to shine brighter and for much, much longer. Sunsets took ages. Our bedroom windows were open to the most stunning view of our fields and those of Farmer Edward's, leading to the River Axe and the hills beyond, dotted with the occasional house or hamlet. We would be woken at dawn's early light by the sound of Richard (one of Edward's sons) whose farm was on our left (about half a mile away) calling in the cattle who had been grazing the fields all night. They would be slowly walked past our house towards Robert's farm (Edward's other son who lived on our right about half a mile away), which housed the milking parlour. After the cows had been milked, they would slowly progress back through the field behind our house grazing as they went. I would always greet them as I opened the back door which was adjacent to one of Edward's fields. "Good morning ladies, keep up the good work." It would take them all day to get back to Richard's farm and I began to tell the time by seeing where the cows were. I was daily reminded of the phrase "when the cows come home" as I could see it in action. I also loved to see the cows in April or May when they first came out to the fields after being in the sheds all winter. They frolicked. They jumped around and pushed each other about with excitement. At first it was odd to see such large animals acting like gambolling lambs, but it made me realise that they too have feelings, senses and emotions.

We also became quite adept at knowing what the weather would be. You could see the weather coming. If it was misty on a spring or summer morning, we would assure the guests that it would be burnt off by about 11 am and we were always right. We also learned to watch the animals. Stupid as they are, sheep will always know when a storm is coming, and if it is they take cover by lying down close to the hedge in the direction of the wind. It's perfect cover for them. If it was windy, we would tell everyone that it would change when the tide at nearby Seaton changed, and we were always right. I don't know how we knew this, but we sort of picked it up by being country people and seeing the weather every day. We lived right in the Axe Valley, with the seaside town of Seaton being a few miles from our house in an almost direct line. The wind would whip up the valley in the winter and whistle around the house. When there were winter storms, the wind was particularly strong and fierce as there was nothing in the way, no other buildings were in the way of the wind. I would lie in bed and hear it almost beating around the house, reminding myself

169

that the house had been standing for more than 150 years and the wind hadn't knocked it over yet. Far more peaceful were the autumn mornings when the mist would lie low in the valley - full of mellow fruitfulness.

If you stood in our hen run and turned your head slightly to the right, a large white house came into view. This was Shute House. The local legend about Shute House was that it had apparently been built by a local big wig in anticipation of a visit from George IV, and it had been built on 'standing corn', fields of which had been set aside to feed the local population. The building of the house had therefore deprived the locals of their corn, and a curse had subsequently been put on the family, that no male heir would ever be born to them again. I have no idea about the veracity of this claim or the curse, but the family did not have a male heir until late into the 20th century. One of the heiresses of the family had married a Spiller, and our house and the land on which it stood was part of her dowry. George IV never did visit the house.

We would always rise very early in the summer. Summer mornings were the best. The day was peaceful and quiet and full of potential. Of course, there was plenty of birdsong. We had a nesting box on the front of the garage and it would always be taken in the spring by a sparrow who would sing his heart out looking for a mate. We had a family of goldcrests who lived in the hedge outside the back door and we really knew summer had begun when the swallows returned. They would arrive every year, swooping around us in the lake field and setting up home in Trotter's Bottom with the pigs. They made nests from mud and sticks which they managed to glue to the wall in perfect little semi circles. Little works of art. I would often find five minutes to gaze in wonder as the adults would hurry back and forth once their chicks were hatched, carrying tiny bundles of grubs and worms to their ever-hungry brood. Sila would watch them too. Waiting patiently by the upturned door which provided ventilation for the pigs and a perfect perch for her by a small square window which the birds would incessantly fly through. She would just sit and wait. A silent assassin.

I never wore a watch at Spillers. I told the time by the sun or the weather, or the position of the cows in the next field. Or whether guests were arriving or leaving. And besides, it didn't matter what the time was. I didn't really go anywhere else or have to be anywhere else. Therein lies a blessing and a curse. I didn't recognise my neighbour Sarah when she came into the tearoom to enquire about the wood chippings we sold from the carpark. (The wood chipping was the result of our nosiness. Trees that formed part of the hedge line were regularly pruned as they tended to grow near and often across the telephone lines along the road. One day, the guys were pruning the trees in our own carpark and turning the twigs into wood chip.

Sensing another revenue stream, we asked what they intended to do with it. Once we realised they just needed somewhere to dump it, we proffered our carpark and every week they'd come along with another load of chippings, which we exchanged for tea and biscuits. Merryck, sensing another food stream got the biscuits. The wood chip pile grew and grew into a huge mound which we sold for £1per bag. It was a fill-your-own-bag scheme and it was very popular even when the pile had been there for a couple of wet seasons and had mushrooms or fungi growing out of it.) The reason I didn't recognise Sarah was because she didn't live in my kitchen. I rarely saw another room for years. Once I had recognised her and realised she was a hairdresser I made sure she was part of my life. I wasn't much of a glamourous type even before Spillers, but once at Spillers and living amongst people whose idea of glamour was a new boiler suit, it became even less of an issue. But hair still needs to be cut, and nothing could be more perfect than strolling across the fields to Sarah's house (my nearest neighbour, but still half a mile away) and having a haircut in return for our spare eggs which she would sell from the honesty box outside her front door.

We went gleaning every year. Edward seemed to have land all over Musbury village and some years some of his fields were planted with maize. After harvesting we would go in and pick up the cobs that had been left behind, placing each one in a sack that we carried on our backs. Some of the fields were acres in size and we walked up and down the rows picking up a single cob here, another one there until the sack was full and we'd go back to Brenda to collect a new sack. It was back breaking work, but worth it to see hear the pigs grunting with happiness tucking into the cobs later on.

People have asked me since how did we do it? How did we manage to work so hard? We never went anywhere empty handed and we never sat down. Well, very rarely. After the first five years we took it slightly easier and quite possibly had a tea break in the afternoon. But you could guarantee that as soon as you sat down with a cuppa, someone would turn up to check in and you'd be back on your feet serving them whilst they sat in the chair you had so recently occupied. We never had trouble sleeping, even when it was boiling hot. We were constantly on the verge of exhaustion. Our favourite quote to describe bedtime comes from Thomas Hardy's Far from the Madding Crowd and concerns the shepherd Gabriel Oak. "In the time it took a man not used to manual labour to decide on which side to lie his head, Gabriel Oak was fast asleep." That was us, every night.

The hospitality sector is hard, hard work. You have to be on call all the time. With a smile on your face. No matter how you were feeling, happy, sad, annoyed, anxious, tired, it didn't matter. You had to give everything to your guests. I always have that in mind whenever I'm in anyone's restaurant, café or B&B now. And smallholding is hard, hard work. The animals don't care if it's Christmas Day, you've got a cold, a broken leg or a hangover. They still need to be fed, milked, cleaned out, cared for. There's no time off.

I did an awful lot of cleaning. I cleaned the same rooms pretty much every day and did an awful lot of laundry. Actually, Keith did quite a bit of the laundry. He was fairly obsessed with the doing the washing and happily did load after load of sheets and towels, hanging them out on the lines he had put up stretching from the garage to the hen house. In quieter moments in the Tearoom, I would tell Polly (Chris and Sue's daughter who was one of our first and longest lasting employees), "Watch this, we're going to have some fun." Keith was (and still is) paranoid about leaving washing out in the rain. I'd call up the stairs, "It's spitting," and stand back. Seconds later, Keith would come tearing through the kitchen rushing out to bring in the washing as though it was on fire.

I did all the ironing though. After realising it takes a full half hour to properly iron a kingsize duvet with a normal iron, we invested in a steam iron, and eventually a large flat pressing machine which fused all the poppers on most of the duvets until I got the hang of it. I would spend at least three hours a day ironing laundry. I have not ironed a single thing since the day I left.

I never wore anything except the Spillers Uniform. A green polo shirt with Spillers Farm embossed on the front, trousers and wellies. The wellies were ubiquitous. Not Hunters. Us country types laughed at people with Hunter wellies. They were for the townies. We would buy the sturdiest wellies we could find at the nearby country stores Mole Avon in Axminster. They had to last at least one winter, possibly two and were essential. Wellies were the footwear of choice from September to at least May, (some years even July). And the fact that I was in wellies made me realise how much I had changed. In my twenties when I lived in London, I had a friend whose family home was in the Kent countryside. Visiting them one weekend and heading out for a walk, her mum handed me a pair of wellies. I refused to wear them and carried them under my arm. Now, I lived in wellies. I had changed.

DUBBY, OR THE MOST PHOTOGRAHED DOG IN DEVON

The most important member of our staff, and certainly the most memorable (if the TripAdvisor reviews were anything to go by). I also call him 'The Most Photographed Dog in Devon' as virtually everyone who passed through our doors wanted to photograph him. It became so common that if anyone so much as lifted their hand to their face (this was pre-selfie days), for Merryck it was 'showtime'. He would come to life, sit properly, look cute at that person and pose. It was all he could do to stop himself doing 'jazz paws'.

He was a very good-looking, very white/blonde dog and as with most Retrievers he had a permanent smile on his face. I'm hardly surprised. He had the most fantastic life. He never wore a lead, he was never left alone and he had his own personal swimming pool in the form of the lake. He spent the day lying down, taking himself from table to table in the breakfast room and then later the tearoom, making sure everyone got a piece of him (and he in turn got a piece of what they were eating). If any of our B&B guests wanted to stretch their legs when they arrived and go for a walk, we would tell them: "Take the dog. Follow him. He'll show you the way." And he would. He would trot off, tail high, glancing over his shoulder to make sure they were following and he'd lead them through the fields to the nearby river, before returning everyone safely home.

He was the central character of all the animals and was the most emotionally intelligent of them all. He walked slowly through the neighbours' large herd of cows, taking a wide berth of most of them, so as not to startle them. He let our cat Sila share his bed and eat from his bowl. Our orphan lambs would often confuse him for their mothers (he being the same shape, size and colour as they) and he would let them headbutt his belly as they searched for a non-present teat. He was never aggressive. The closest he ever came to aggression was when he was eating a bone on the tearoom lawns. One of our hens (we called her Atilla – Atilla the Hen) was quite the free-ranger and she would wander far and wide, including the Tearoom lawns. She started to approach Merryck and his bone and he lifted one side of his mouth - Presley-like - to show her one of his fangs, as if to say, "I've got teeth Atilla, certainly more teeth than you've got." She stopped and changed direction.

He belonged to us and everyone. He was everyone's friend. There was not a person or another creature that he didn't like (except Mr Darcy. He was petrified of Mr Darcy as you can probably tell from the photo on page 69). One summer he became an honorary member of a gang of kids who teamed up for the holidays on the caravan site and called themselves The Spillers Farm Five. Merryck was the number five and whilst they were on holiday he would leave the house as soon as he'd had breakfast and head over to the caravan site, where he would sit outside of the one caravan waiting for at least one of the gang to get up and start playing. He did this for a few days before he was actually invited into the caravan. We barely saw him that week. I'm not even sure he came home on some nights! I can see him sitting in the middle of them all as they posed for their final photograph and it makes me very happy to think of him being part of someone's childhood memories.

He wasn't a natural country dog. We got him from a breeder in Watford whilst we were still living in London. But we always had the intention of moving to the countryside with him. It took a little longer than we planned, but he was in situ by the time he was two. And he loved it. He took to countryside life like a dog to the farm born. Some of my favourite memories are of watching Keith and Merryck go out to shoot. Keith was what he liked to call a 'rough shooter' and you couldn't get more rough than Keith's shooting. The pheasants and ducks were pretty safe around Keith. You can imagine them saying to each other, "Watch out below, there's a bloke with a dog and a gun. Oh, hang on, it's just that lousy shot Trayling, we'll be fine." What Keith meant by rough shooting, was that it was not part of an organised 'stand here whilst the birds are driven in our direction by lots of peasants scaring them out of their habitats and hiding places' kind of shoot. He liked to describe himself as 'a dog walker with a gun' and as previously mentioned – that is a lot less dangerous than it sounds!

During the winter months of the shooting season, he and Merryck would go shooting most afternoons. For a dog from Watford, Merryck was obsessed with the gun. Especially the sound of it being shot. It was amazing to see his instinct at work. He was never trained and as far as we had known he'd never seen a gun. He'd spent his life prior to Spillers on the mean streets of Kensal Green (much meaner than the gentrified place it has now become, stuffed with mortgaged millionaires), a place not known for its pheasant shoots. But as soon as he saw Keith's shotgun he was transfixed. He would immediately leave whatever he was doing (even if it was food) and rush to the back door gripped with some massive adrenaline rush. "IT'S THE THING! IT'S THE THING!", we imagined him shouting, "MAKE IT MAKE THE NOISE! MAKE THE NOISE! I LOVE THE NOISE!" From there I would watch as Keith and he would head out across the fields, Merryck gripping the hedge line, sniffing out any poor bird that happened to be taking cover there. How he knew how to do this was a mystery. Some instinctive Retriever behaviour from generations back was still pulsing through his born-in-Watford blood.

I say Retriever, but he was more of a Leaver than a Retriever. If Keith ever managed to bring anything down from the skies by actually shooting it rather than shooting around, or near it, Merryck's instincts stopped right there. He would look at the dead bird near him and look back at Keith as if to say, "you shot it. You pick it up!" He would retrieve wood though, the benefits of which I have still to discover. Farmer Edward's fields regularly flooded in the winter (being on a floodplain, near a river and subject to the south west's famously wet autumns, winters, some summers and yep, most springs), and this would leave tree branches of all shapes, sizes and weights floating in massive puddles in the fields just behind ours. Where these branches actually came from is also a mystery. They were never in the fields when it was dry, but after a lot of rain there was always a big lump of wood floating around in a puddle. Merryck would like nothing more in the winter than to charge into the puddle – sometimes deep enough for him to swim in the centre – and drag the log back to us, only for us to throw it back in and for him to happily charge back in and repeat the process ad nauseum.

But for Merryck nothing surpassed a stone. Medium sized preferably, more pebble than gravel, he was never happier than when he was carrying a stone about in his mouth. Don't ask me where this obsession came from (or why we never seemed able to stop it), but he loved stones. They fascinated him. If I was ever weeding our larger-than-I-would-have-made-them flower borders or especially the large gravel driveway (both of which I did on my hands and knees – no making life easier by spraying weeds from a container for us), Merryck's head would suddenly appear over my shoulder his face bearing an intense expression which I knew said "Got any stones? Go on, throw me a stone". And I would. I'd take a small stone and throw it a couple of feet away. Merryck would trot over, gently pick it up and hold it at the front of his mouth and after a while, he'd lie down and pop the stone back on the ground at his paws, gazing at it as if it was the most exquisite diamond. I'm sure there are many of you who are astounded, affronted and faintly amazed that someone who calls herself a dog lover would actively throw stones for her dog (and with hindsight, it does sound absolutely nuts), but he never swallowed one, never damaged himself and I never actually aimed them at him. He had plenty of normal toys as well, it's not like he ever only played with stones, but he especially loved the stones on nearby Seaton beach. His two great loves would come together in one at Seaton. Gateway to the beautiful Jurassic Coast, Seaton is pebbly and stony: the great sweep of the bay covered in hundreds of thousands of lovely stones washed smooth by the tides washing the shore over millennia. Out of season, when dogs were allowed on the beach, Merryck was in his heaven at Seaton. He would charge down to the sea and plough into the waves. He loved to swim. Every day included a swim for Merryck. If he didn't swim in the lake, he made sure he would swim along the river if we went for a walk. In fact, before we went to Spillers, we had a canal boat holiday where Merryck spent the entire four days swimming in the canal behind the boat. We kept trying to get him into the longboat with us, but he was having none of it.

Once he was a few feet out in the sea, past the breakers, he would start swimming horizontal to the shore and staring at us. We'd know what he was asking for. Both picking up a handful of stones, we would then throw them, one-by-one a few yards in front of him and he would continue to swim in that direction, only looking back at us if the stream of stones stopped. He would swim for ages as long as the stones continued and I think he might have been one of those dogs you hear about who do these mammoth swims, like say to the Isle of Wight. Merryck would have swum from Seaton to France if someone had been in a boat in front of him throwing stones in the water.

He was the gentlest creature. He ate incredibly slowly. And I don't mean for a dog he ate incredibly slowly. He really, really ate incredibly slowly. He savoured every mouthful. He would pick up a piece of kibble, chew it thoughfully and – if we were in the vicinity – look round at us as if to say: "Hmm, chicken and rice again, my favourite." Sils (our cat, those of you still reading from the early chapters may remember her swimming ability) might come along whilst he was eating, and (having already wolfed down her food) would stick her head in his bowl and start munching away. If she did this, he would remove his head and wait until she'd had enough before sampling each morsel again.

As with all our other animals, his name changed over the years. What started as Merryck became something completely different. We started to nickname him 'tuppence' as a term of endearment which got shortened to dubbins, and eventually Dubby or Dubs for short. He answered to it all.

They were quite remarkable in some ways Dubs and Sils. Sometimes she was more dog than he. Before we had pets I had assumed that if it would be our dog that might drink out of the toilet. It has been known for a dog to do that. But, at Spillers Farm if was our cat that did that, especially after a recent flush. In a further episode of 'What I heard by my AGA,' I bring you a story called, 'What my cat does in the loo'. I heard a tearoom customer enter the loo that was near the kitchen.

Customer: "Hello! What are you doing here?"

Sila (I like to imagine she'd sound exactly like a sarcastic Lauren Bacall): "I'm waiting until you flush, so that I can have a drink. You know how to flush don't you"

Of course, the customer didn't speak cat, so she had no idea why Sila was sitting apparently innocently in the corner of the smallest room in the house.

As with our laissez-faire attitude to our dogs' obsession with the stones, you must be wondering how we could leave our poor cat so thirsty as to have to stoop to drinking from the bog. There was always fresh water available, but she obviously always preferred the likely aftertaste of Toilet Duck. For a minute there I was worried I might have lost the Health and Safety Officers in the readership, but I'm pretty sure I lost them some time ago discussing Sils habit of sleeping in the cupboards.

Merryck nearly caught a fox once. I think the fox must've been very ill or exceptional old. It wasn't running that fast, but once Merryck had seen it he was off, chasing it down as fast as he could. And once he did that fox was in trouble, that would be it for the fox, he was going to tear it limb from limb. That might have what was going on in his mind when they made the film of his life, but in reality, he caught up with the fox and started running along next to it, glancing at it sideways now and again, as if to say, "This is brilliant. Great fun. Where are we going?"

He was just a soft with a bone. Not one to guard his food, you could easily take a bone right out of his mouth. If you did, he would just look at you slightly affronted and give you his paw asking for it back. If he got a bit of bone stuck in his teeth, he would come up to you with his mouth open at an odd angle and we'd fish the bit of bone out of one of his back molars. We never had to worry that Merryck would act badly towards any guest. He was the softest creature. Kids crawled all over him. There are quite a few photos of him with the guests' children on his back, pulling on his fur, grasping his tail. And in every photo he is loving every minute of it. One of my friends came to stay for a weekend, with her husband and young Down Syndrome son who was apparently terrified of dogs. After a weekend with Merryck her son declared that he now actually wanted to be a dog.

Whether this meant that he was now obsessed with stones I didn't discover.

His gentleness hid a timid side. He was not a brave dog. More likely to run away from danger and hide behind our legs should anyone have tried to burgle us, he once went on a rescue mission with Keith to fetch some guests from the local pub. Having lost their bearings walking to the pub in Musbury, they rang at closing time telling us they were lost. Equipped with a torch and a quaking Merryck, Keith set out down Dead Horse Lane to show them the way home. Merryck was not at all keen. It was dark, it was scary and he bore a striking resemblance to the closing credits of Dad's

Army as he tremblingly followed Keith looking over his shoulder at me and waiting for rescue.

He had a certain walk that we did most days. Well, he did it most days. Sometimes we took him, in the summer season it was guests that took him. We'd get out of the back field though a gap in the hedge and over the ditch between the fields. (Interestingly dug by local POWs in the Second World War. Very well constructed. Very straight. Very Prussian.) Down Dead Horse Lane, where, more often than not, we would meet The Major. The Major (that's what we called him. In 10 years I'm not sure we ever found out his actual name) owned a field along the lane which he seemingly just used for an enormous bonfire every 5th November for his family. As September turned into October it would start to form, until by early November a great pyramid of wood had been assembled. On the night in question, you could easily see the smoke and fireworks from our back door. A free firework display on the doorstep. What could be better?

The Major wore a large trilby and a bushy, white moustache. He looked like a cross between one of Dad's Army and The Major in Fawlty Towers – hence the nickname – smoked like a trouper and had a big booming voice not unlike Brian Blessed. He was the kind of man who would find it perfectly natural to call everybody 'Old Boy', even the women. Once past the Major we'd turn onto the East Devon Way towards the white farmhouse where Merryck's girlfriend lived. Trixie was a dog of unknown breed who seemed to bark at every other dog who passed her way but loved Merryck. They'd play and frolic for a bit before we moved on and she would wait for his return on our way home. Once when she was on heat she followed us all the way home, pushing her nether regions into Merryck's snout, which he completely ignored and seemed a bit confused by all her pleading prancing.

We had not intended to get him neutered. We intended to breed him and keep a bitch (who we would call Mollie) to spend his life with. But he rather ruined that plan one week in the September after we moved to Spillers. Never knowing when customers would arrive, we had to keep our gates open, and three times in one week we noticed Merryck had gone missing. After being frantic with worry for a while the first time and beginning mentally to design 'Missing Dog' posters, we received a phone call from someone in the village, "We've got your dog," and he was happily fetched. After the third time, we didn't worry. We just waited for the phone call. He'd obviously smelt some bitch on heat in the village and wandered off in search of true love. It was then we had to phone the vet. "Oh, I know your dog. A large white one? Saw him on the road this morning heading into the village."

And so there would never be a Mollie. On the subject of animals we never had, we considered getting some cattle. We thought about getting two

Dexter bulls. The smallest native breed of cattle in the British Isles, the Dexter is a hardy, stocky breed that we thought would give us a change from the all-pork diet. We intended getting two – Ant and Dec – but thought the pressure of making sure they always stood the right way round would be too much. We had a fascinating visit from one couple who brought their Harris Hawk away with them and he stayed (for free) in one of our sheds. Keith became very interested in the hawk and how he flew and exercised. It seemed like the sort of activity that was busier in the winter than the summer and we briefly considered getting a hawk to fly around Dartmoor during our slightly less busy months. We were going to call him Rolf. Probably just as well that we didn't.

For a short while we adopted a homing pigeon, whom we called Gregory Peck. At the height of the summer, pigeon fanciers would gather at nearby at the costal cliffs nearby – Beer Heights – and set their pigeons free. They – presumably – would drive back to Yorkshire and await the arrival of their birds. Sometimes a few – the least able - would not make it back and one of these landed on our garage roof, looked confused, and settled down to live with the hens. For a few days he hung around, dodging Sila who spent her days stalking him, and making himself very much at home in the hen house. Although he was friendly enough to eat out of our hands we knew he was not really our pet and we could not keep him for long. Being idiots who had no idea how to identify a homing pigeon, we thought the best thing would be to take him away from the farm and let him go, hoping that this time he would reset his internal sat nav and fly home properly. So, we took him to the River Axe which intersected Farmer Edward's field just below ours thinking that the river might be a good navigational tool for him and threw him into the air. He flew high into the air, circled once and then again and we watched with hope in our hearts that his homing skills had clicked in and then felt our hope disappear as he resolutely turned towards Spillers and settled back on the roof leaving us to trudge back through the fields. A few days later we noticed he had gone, so he either did make it back, or he is still living feral in the Axe Valley. Probably with some hens.

Merryck had the best life any dog could ever desire. Never on his own, never in kennels if we went away (we were fortunate in having a long list of people who wanted to house and dog sit), never on a lead even, he lived the life of Riley. Growing older with all that space around him he matured into a gloriously happy dog with an enviable life. But, all things must come to an end and eventually it became clear that we were unable to maintain the Spillers lifestyle and it was time to move on.

LEAVING THE DREAM

By 2015 we had been at Spillers for ten years. My parents and Keith's father were ageing and needing more care from us. It became difficult to manage helping them and running the business, and Keith was coming up to retirement age, so we decided to make 2015 our last year. It was a tricky year to manage. We had to sell the business as a going concern, but also run down the livestock at the same time as there was no way of knowing if the people who might buy Spillers might want to have pigs, sheep etc.

So that spring, for the first time in many years we

didn't have lambs. It was a beautiful spring, but poorer for the lack of little gambolling balls of woolly fluff bouncing around. We sold our latest boar – Delboy – to another smallholder in Exeter and took the last litter of piglets to market when they were ready, until Marlene was the last pig standing. And eventually, even she was gone. A sadness settled over Spillers and over the ground that the pigs had made their own, where they had rooted, played, splashed in mud baths and grunted with happiness. To me it looked barren and desolate.

"Do you know how wonderful this place is?" Carl said. Jayne and Carl were the only people who came to view Spillers Farm. It had been on the market for six months and we had despaired of anyone wanting to take it on. We were just about to change estate agents due to the lack of viewings, but they agent had begged us to give him just one more chance with this viewing. He said they were very keen.

He was right. I knew Jayne and Carl would buy it from the minute they walked through the tearoom door. They had been following my blog on the website and had clearly fallen in love with the place before they saw it. The thing is, we did know how wonderful it was, even when it was seemingly barren and desolate. They could see what we had seen that first damp and dreary November morning when we first laid eyes on Spillers. And it looked a lot better than then. They could see the potential.

Even though they were not there they could see the sheep and pigs and were as keen as we were to keep it all going.

I am delighted to say that they did buy it, lock stock and barrel, and six months after they put in an offer, we were off, packing our belongings into a small truck and moving 15 minutes' drive away into Somerset. As they bought everything – crockery, cutlery, furniture, bedding - we walked away with just our own furniture. One bed, one sofa, and our clothes. It was like we were moving out of a one bed flat, not a five bedroomed farmhouse! They are still running it today and judging by the Trip Advisor reviews, doing a marvellous job. It would seem that we sold Spillers to ourselves in a way. Jayne and Carl looked quite a lot like us, except he was taller than Keith and she was slightly smaller than I. How much they looked like us can be illustrated by my mother's comment when I showed her a photo of Jayne and Carl boating round the lake a few months after they moved in. "What are you doing on the lake?" said my mother. We had indeed found our rightful successors.

We only really returned to Spillers once. Merryck died in October 2017 after a happy and peaceful retirement in Somerset. We asked Jayne and Carl if they would let us scatter some of his ashes at the lake where he spent so much of his time. They graciously said yes and when we arrived, they met us at the door with the words, "We are constantly on our feet, we never sit down and there is just not enough time to do everything!" We smiled wryly. We know. You're living the dream. Sorry about that.

EPILOGUE

As you get older, you look back at your life and realise that certain periods of time were the best. You think, if only I'd known then how good that time was. If only I'd known it was the best time of my life I might have enjoyed it more. We knew Spillers was good. We knew it was the best time of our lives at the time we were living it. For the ten - almost 11 - years I was at Spillers I wrote a blog. I updated it at least monthly, sometimes weekly, depending on what was happening. The blog is long gone, but here is the last one, dated 14th November 2015. We left Spillers on 19th November 2015.

A Last Look at Spillers

The boxes are nearly packed. The pictures are off the wall. It all looks quite empty. But it isn't of course.

When I look in the tearoom, I don't see the piles of boxes. I see the thousands of people who have enjoyed a Spillers farm breakfast and I can hear Keith telling hundreds of them how that there's no money in pigs. I see people on holiday, laughing in the sun and sharing a cream tea, arguing about whether it's cream or jam first. I see the tearoom door open on a beautiful summer's day and people sitting in the garden having a pot of tea and a piece of apple cake. I see a young Merryck going from table to table making sure everyone gets a bit of his company. I see Atilla the Hen (versions one and two) extreme free ranging and snatching some crumbs from under the tables. I see the Christmas lunches we did in the very early days and the panic that hit us as the power shorted as soon as we put the dishwasher on! (Nobody noticed....isn't wine wonderful,,,,?)

When I climb the stairs to the bedrooms, I don't see empty rooms. I see the thousands of guests that we have had the privilege of hosting over the past 11 years. I see faces young and old who arrived as strangers and left as friends, some of whom will be friends for life. I hear the laughter we've shared with most of them and the shocking and tragic stories that we've heard from some, that have made us realise how fortunate we are and made us incredibly thankful to be alive.

As I look out of my bedroom window, I not only say goodbye to the most fantastic and beautiful view in the world, but also, I can see how the lake has changed over the years from a basic hole in the ground to a wonderful place of majestic and natural beauty, most of which has just emerged from the ground without us planting hardly a thing. I think about the wildlife that is now resident: moorhens and coots, as well as the visitors, wild ducks, an occasional kingfishers, geese and – of course – the swans. How will they fare next year I wonder?

It's quiet as I gaze at the garden, but I can hear Kellogg crowing, not only first thing in the morning, but pretty continuously all day! I can her his crow quickly taken up by Cornflake – but at a much higher pitch. I hear the chirruping of the chicks that we hatched and see the ones that hatched naturally, popping out from under their mother's feathers. I see the ducks waddling down from the lake to see if the hens have left any crumbs from breakfast, all except for Limpy our oldest duck who broke her leg years ago and now only makes the journey to the lake once a day. I can hear her now quacking at the departing ducks telling them not to be long as she'll get lonely.

Gazing out at the lake field I see our 40 or so lambs and sheep that we've had over the years gambolling, running, chomping grass, playing with and following Merryck. I hear them bleating to be bottle fed and I can almost feel them suckling my fingers. But most of all, I hear myself calling "PF!", "PF!" for PFS (Pretty Fluffy Sheep) and seeing her break from the flock and come running over for a cuddle. I can still feel her wool tickling my face as I bury it in her fluffy neck and breathe in the warm, lanolin smell of living, breathing wool.

Walking into Trotter's Bottom, the pig sty, is the most bittersweet of all, of course. But they're all still here. I can hear piglets grunting, squealing and playing, chasing each other on their tiny little trotters that look so much like a ballerina en pointe. I see Cassie out in the field playing piggy "tig" with her first of many, many litters. I wander out by the veg garden and Marlene wanders over the see if I've dug up any weeds for her. She greets me with lots of grunts. She was always the most talkative. I give her a good scratch with the head of an old yard brush and she shakes her head in gratitude. Rodders, the largest – yet most lovable – pig in the world is lying on his side in the sun giving me his trotter as a sign that he'd like a belly rub please.

So as I take one last, long look at Spillers it's not empty at all. It is full. It is full of the sights sounds and smells of the best years of my life. I see it all. I see the animals that we've loved and cared for. I see the little one born here and the ones that didn't make it. I see all the people who came through our doors and shared our lives, even if it was just for a very short time.

But, most of all, I see myself. I see how much I've changed. Spillers Farm has turned me from a City Girl into a Country Woman. I may be leaving Spillers, but it will never leave me.

ABOUT THE AUTHOR

Bridget Trayling lives in Somerset with her husband
Keith and their dog Arthur.

She still wears wellies.

Printed by Amazon Italia Logistica S.r.l.
Torrazza Piemonte (TO), Italy